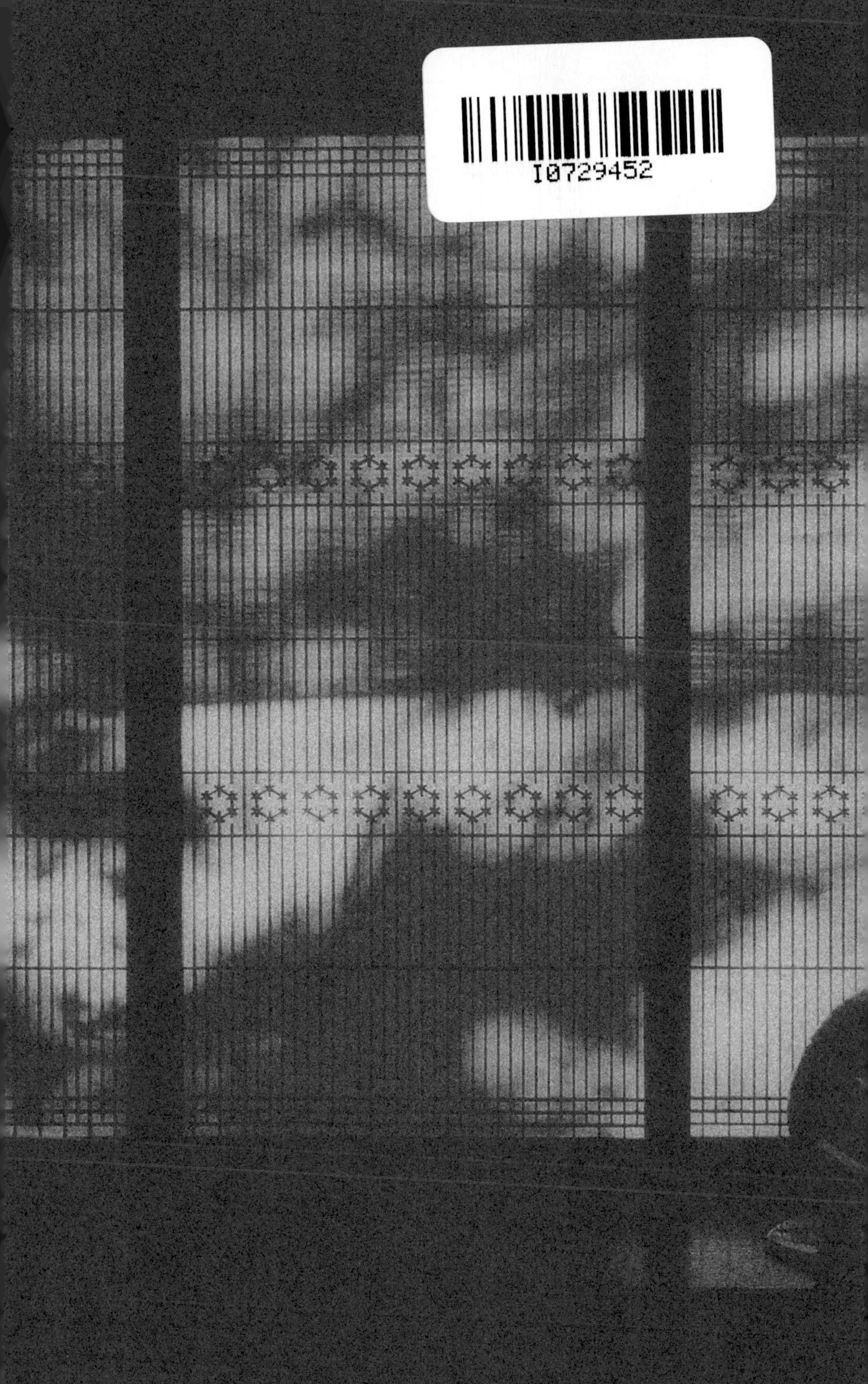

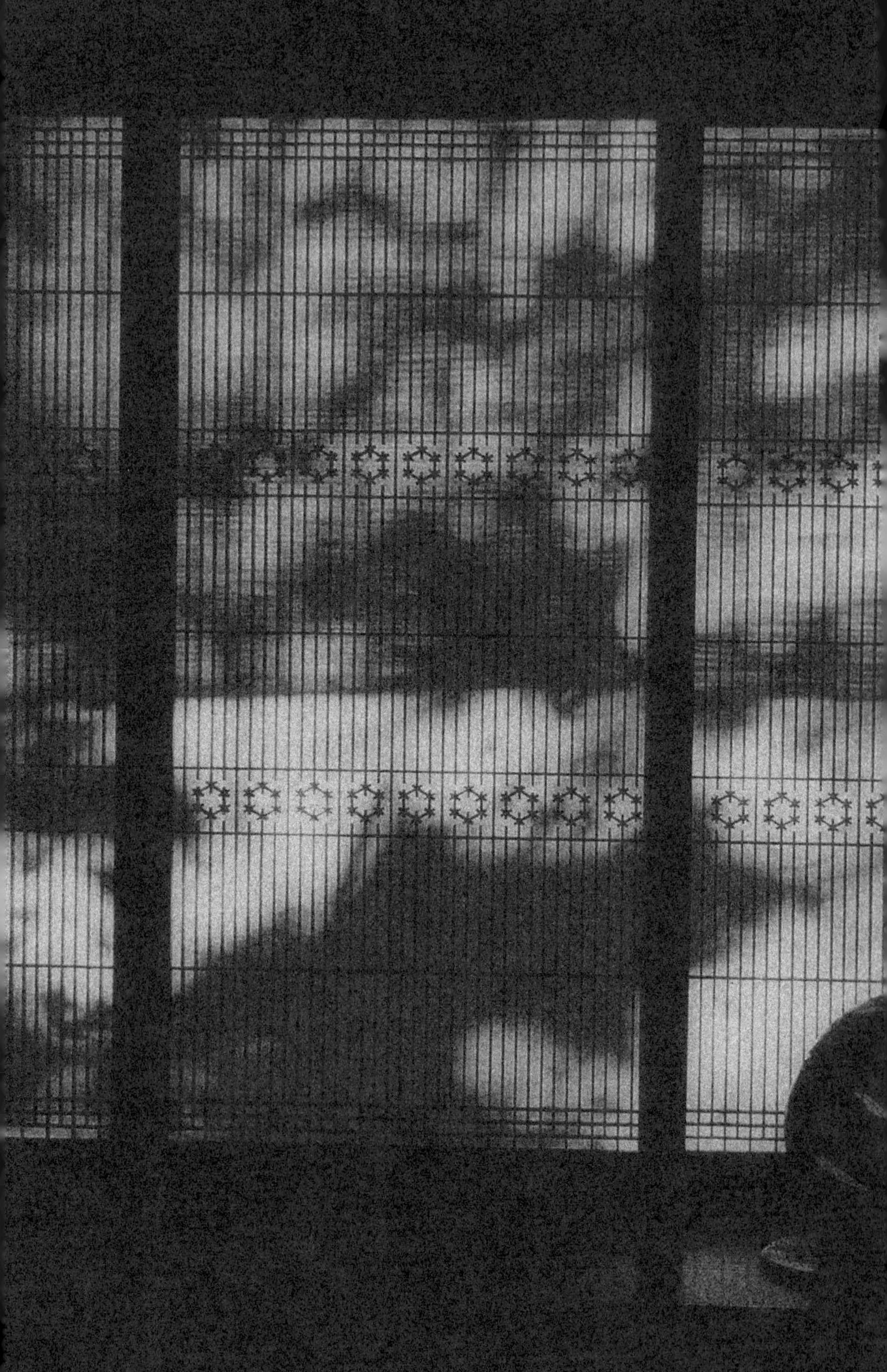

Illusory Dwellings

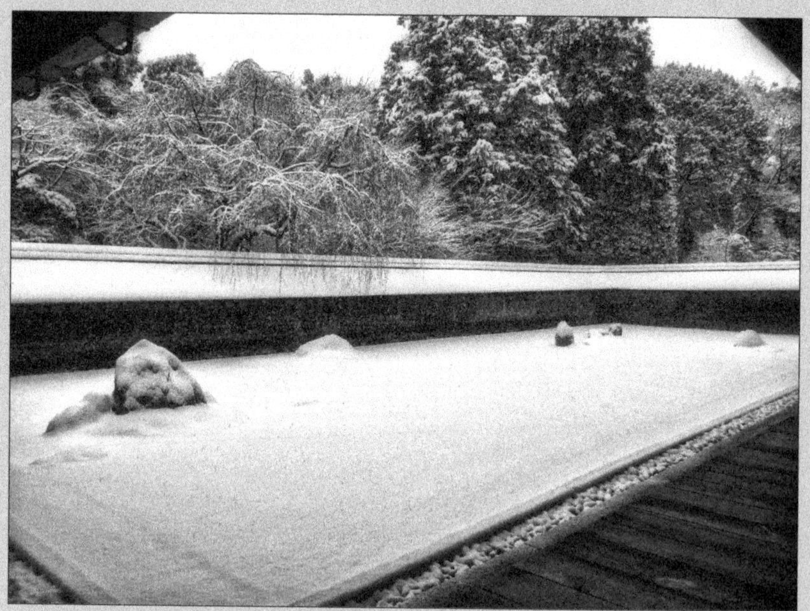

Ryōan-ji.

Illusory Dwellings

AESTHETIC MEDITATIONS IN KYOTO

Allen S. Weiss

Stone Bridge Press • *Berkeley, California*

Published by
Stone Bridge Press
P.O. Box 8208, Berkeley, CA 94707
sbp@stonebridge.com • www.stonebridge.com

Following Japanese convention, Japanese family names are followed by given names, except in cases where people are known otherwise outside Japan, for example D. T. Suzuki.

The original version of this book appeared as *Guide anachronique de Kyoto,* published in 2023 by Éditions Arléa (Paris).

Cover photograph by Allen S. Weiss: Kinkaku-ji (The Temple of the Golden Pavilion), Kyoto.

All photographs in this book are by Allen S. Weiss except the following: Jōmon ceramic vase, © Metropolitan Museum of Art, page 21; Tea performance with Yumi Mukai, © Courtesy Ullman Photography, page 39; Yagi Kazuo, *Mr. Samsa's Walk,* © Yagi Akira, page 59; Fukami Sueharu, *Upright* (Kitsu), © Courtesy Fukami Sueharu / Hatakeyama Takashi, page 74; Koie Ryōji, *Return to the Earth,* © Utsuwakan Gallery / Koroda Takeru, page 80; Sesshū Tōyō, scroll, Kyoto National Museum (source: Wikimedia Commons), page 124.

Printed in the United States of America.

First printing 2024.

p-ISBN 978-1-61172-083-9
e-ISBN 978-1-61172-967-2

But is there anybody who does not live in an illusory dwelling?
Matsuo Bashō, *Record of an Unreal Dwelling*

CONTENTS

Preface 9

1   Equivocal Thresholds | THE TEA ROOM *19*

2   Other Modernities | THE MUSEUM *35*

3   Perfect Offerings | THE RESTAURANT *83*

4   Untimely Moons | THE GARDEN *105*

5   Tanizaki's Tomb | THE CEMETERY *141*

Endnotes 159

Recommended Readings 178

Acknowledgments 179

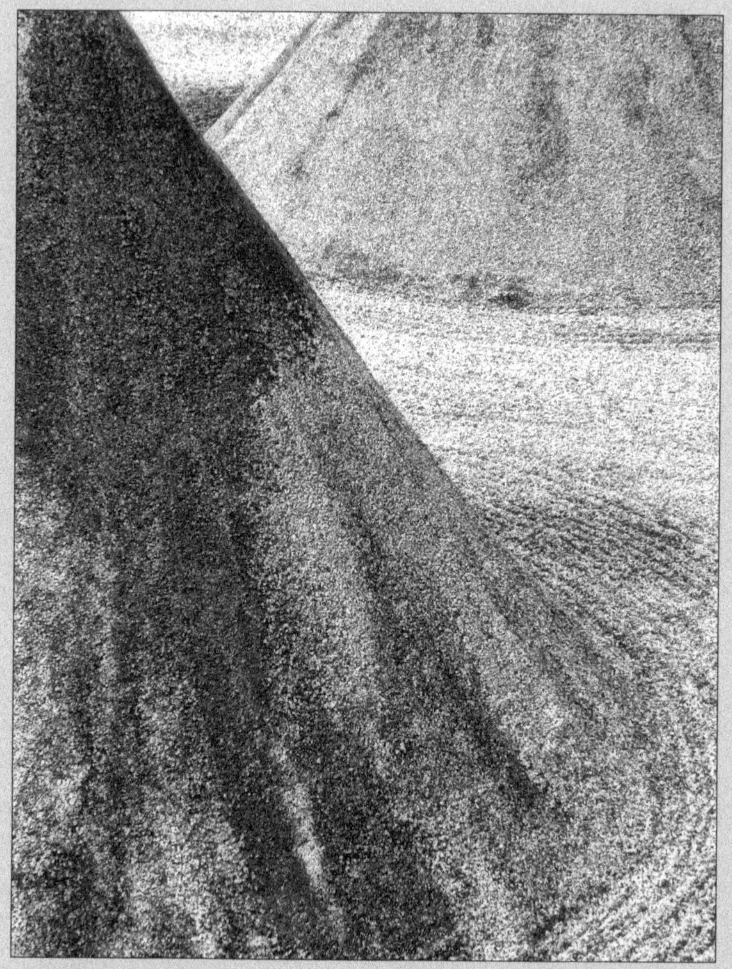

Kamigamo-jinja.

PREFACE

To discover a land is first of all to assemble
all the memories that announced it.
René de Ceccatty, "Lettres de Tokyo"[1]

The celebrated dealer of Japanese art and antiquities James Freeman, who spent four decades in Kyoto, begins an autobiographical essay with the following citation from Rainer Maria Rilke: "We are born, so to speak, provisionally, it doesn't matter where; it is only gradually that we compose, within ourselves, our true place of origin, so that we may be born there retrospectively and each day more definitely."[2] The great Japan scholar Donald Richie cites the same passage in *The Japan Journals*.[3] We travel to confirm or transform—or even create—our identity. A voyage is as much about ourselves as our destinations. We map a city according to our fantasies and desires, and in turn the city frames our lives and inflects our destinies.

A true voyage begins well before departure, and it does not end with homecoming, for a trip is never-ending, both anticipated and perpetually renewed in literature and myth, cuisine and art, reveries and dreams. This is beautifully and profoundly expressed by Ernest Hemingway in the epigraph to *A Moveable Feast*, taken from a letter to a friend: "If you are lucky enough to have lived in Paris as a young man, then wherever you go for the rest of your life, it stays with you, for Paris is a moveable feast."[4] (I was, in fact, one such young man, but that tale will be the subject of another book.) Much travel is really about reading and writing. Charles Darwin, writing of his "habit of energetic industry and concentrated attention," notes in *Voyage of the Beagle*, one of the most influential travelogues ever written: "Everything about which I thought or read was made to bear directly on what I had seen or was likely to see; and this habit of mind was continued during the five years of voyage."[5] Some travel is even about pure fantasy, as epitomized by Raymond Roussel's voyages in his *roulotte*, from which he rarely ventured to see the actual landscape. We prepare by perusing guides and devouring travelogues; during our trips we take notes and photos; afterward this is all distilled into anecdotes and tales, occasionally essays and books, and of course reorganized on shelves of souvenirs and collections, veritable private museums.

Every traveler has particular proclivities. In Japan, some seek the Buddhist Western Paradise, others the world of Hayao Miyazaki's *Spirited Away*; for some the ideal is the meditative calm of a tea pavilion or a Zen temple in the foothills of Kyoto, for others the noisy gregariousness of a jazz club or a sake bar in Tokyo's prodigious Shibuya quarter. We oscillate between varying paradigms: regional, national, international; traditional, modernist, postmodern; the ancient capital Kyoto and the modern capital Tokyo. The itinerant curator and chronicler of the history of curating, Hans Ulrich Obrist, claims that "It is simply impossible to portray a city."[6] It is just as impossible to portray a culture. What does one seek in Japan? Kabuki or Butoh? Bashō or Tanizaki? Hiroshige or Kurosawa? What amalgam, however improbable, guides one's steps? For if the traditional, the modern, and the postmodern are states of mind and not merely stylistic categories, they exist simultaneously and determine radically different facets of one and the same object or event, radically different aspects of ourselves. The distinctions, oppositions, dualisms, bifurcations, aporia, ambiguities, and paradoxes discussed in what follows are often apparent within a single work, image, thought.

What role can a book play in such wanderings? In *The Dharma Bums* (1958)—a sequel to that bible of the Beat generation, *On the Road* (1957)—Jack Kerouac offers a fictive account of the early years of poet and ecologist Gary Snyder, culminating in the summer the narrator spent as a fire lookout in the Sierra Nevada mountain range. This moment was contemporaneous with Snyder's discovery of Zen Buddhism—as for so many of his generation, in great part through the work of philosopher and historian of religion D. T. Suzuki—just before Snyder's first trip to Japan in 1955. The words that Kerouac penned for the quasi-fictive Snyder were prescient: "I'll do a new long poem called 'Rivers and Mountains Without End' and just write it on and on on a scroll and unfold on and on with new surprises and always what went before forgotten, see, like a river, or like one of them real long Chinese silk paintings that show two little men hiking in an endless landscape of gnarled old trees and mountains so high they merge with the fog in the upper silk void. I'll spend three thousand years writing it, it'll be packed full of information on soil conservation, the Tennessee Valley Authority, astronomy, geology, Hsuan Tsung's travels, Chinese painting theory, reforestation, Oceanic ecology and food chains."[7] In fact, Snyder had already begun to write *Rivers and Mountains Without End* in 1956 and didn't complete it until 1996: a Borgesian task, tantamount to reflecting upon the total environment of an entire life.[8] It is also a great lesson concerning the complexity of living across two or more cultures.

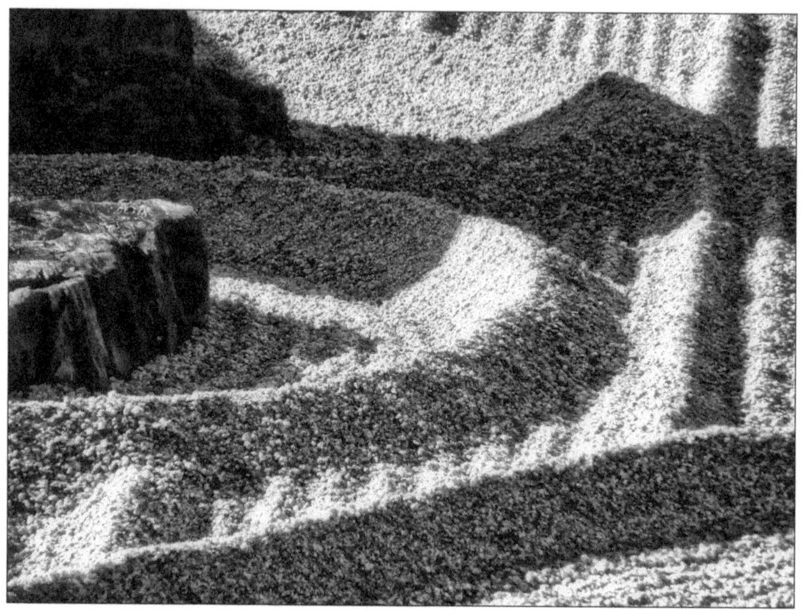

Ryōgen-in.

It has been said that there are two kinds of people: those who divide the world into two kinds of people, and those who don't. Reductive as this may be, I find this exercise useful as a starting point, especially in relation to travel, for I would suggest that the two fundamental categories are those who travel to find themselves and those who travel to lose themselves. Some even manage to find themselves by losing themselves, which is the way of Zen. During his many years spent in Japan during the 1950s and 1960s, Gary Snyder—who might well be considered the American Bashō—learned Japanese, studied Zen Buddhism in Kyoto, and became a practicing Buddhist. His trajectory reminds us that some travelers just pass through, while others leave traces; some are unchanged, while others are transformed.

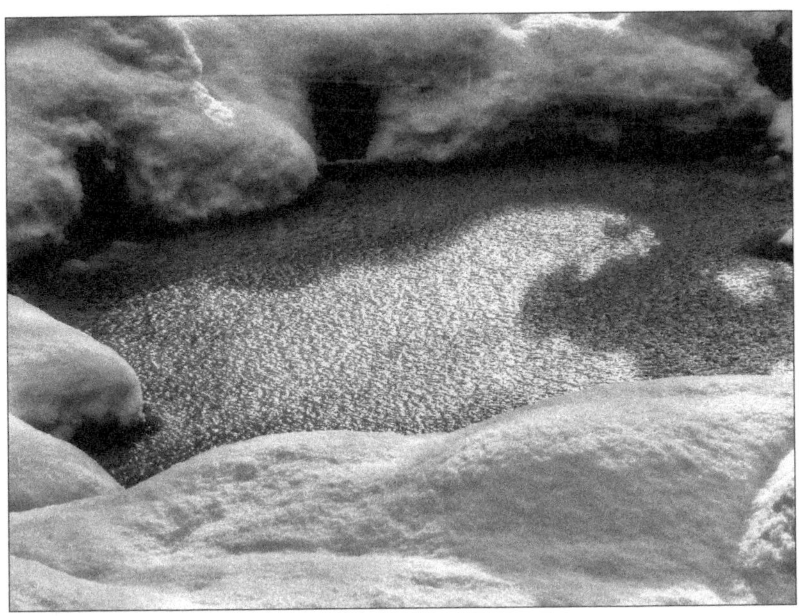

Jikkō-in, Ōhara.

Or maybe we need to divide travelers up differently and say that there are those who seek the familiar while others search for the foreign, strange, mysterious, exotic.

The 19th-century author and naturalist Henry David Thoreau revealed in his masterpiece, *Walden; or, Life in the Woods* (1854), that the greatest wonders of nature may be found in a clearing in the woods or at the edge of the road, literally in one's own back yard. Thoreau, one of the great proponents of New England Transcendentalism—which was profoundly influenced by Japanese, Chinese, and Indian philosophy—taught us how to see the most familiar as profoundly wondrous. A single blade of grass is no less amazing and imposing than a millennial oak. One might add that he also taught us to *hear* the wonders of nature: his diaries reveal that he had perhaps the best ear of the 19th century for the nuances of sound in the natural world, as well as for their translation into language. We need to transform our seeing and listening, experience the proximate as exotic, recast the familiar as foreign: detailed observation and vivid imagination are forms of travel.

One dear friend, the late Lawrence R. Schehr—with whom I shared many literary and gastronomic adventures in Paris, London, New York—was a specialist in both 19th-century French literature and queer culture. He had more than once done the Grand Tour of Europe—the cultural itinerary that was a rite of passage for young men (and occasionally women), often aspiring writers or painters, from the mid-17th through the late 19th century—each time traveling with a set of vintage Baedeker guides, in an attempt to align his vision with that of a 19th-century traveler. His journeys through Europe were thus a form of time travel, articulated by the travel writings of Stendhal, Goethe, Heine, Dickens, Henry James, Robert Louis Stevenson. The advent of the automobile and the airplane have radically changed the nature of the Grand Tour, democratizing it to the point that during the summer months many of the city centers of the great cultural capitals of Europe, not to mention Kyoto, can hardly be approached due to the masses of tourists. Yet this transformation of travel holds certain advantages. Hans Ulrich Obrist explains how as a teenager in the 1980s he took advantage of the Interrail pass to ride night train after night train in order to crisscross Europe and interview the artists he most admired. "Those were apprenticeship and journeyman years, a European Grand Tour."[9] The project of contemplating ancient masterpieces by long dead masters,

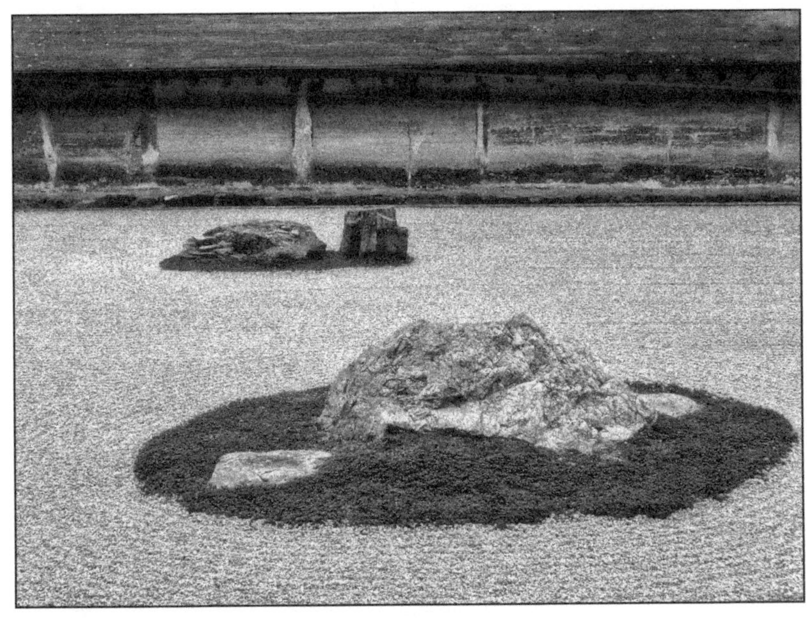

Ryōan-ji.

which had previously demanded many months, much wealth, and certain danger, was updated by Obrist as an express trip on limited funds to see the most recent works by preeminent living artists.

Illusory Dwellings concerns what few guide books attempt: there is little need for yet another book to suggest *what* to see in Kyoto, but it might be of interest to present some thoughts on *how* to see in this ancient and still ebullient cultural capital.[10] Following upon my books *Zen Landscapes* and *The Grain of the Clay*, I have not spent three thousand years, nor even the forty that it took Snyder to compose *Rivers and Mountains Without End*, in writing *Illusory Dwellings*, but I plan to include information on architecture

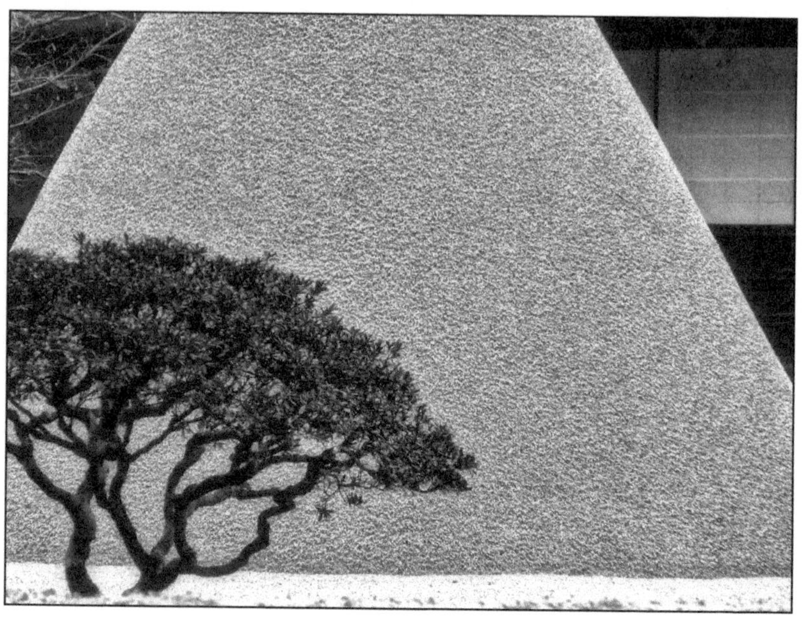

Ginkaku-ji.

and gardens, ceramics and cuisine, the wind in the pines, the ever-present yet hidden void, several full moons, and a generous amount of sake.

It is quite difficult to eschew habits, rituals, obsessions. Yet one should not prepare too well for a journey, for at the core of travel must be serendipity. Too-rigorous preparation is like putting on a pair of blinders. Better to sensitize one's vision and quicken one's imagination than to make overabundant lists and reservations. Successful travel necessitates that at times the veneer of erudition must dissolve, to reveal depths of ignorance that are synonymous with openness. Such is the principle of a voyager's *docta ignorantia*.

◆ ◆ ◆

A garden or a city is a state of mind as much as a physical locale. In *Flights*, the Nobel Prize–winning author and veteran traveler Olga Tokarczuk warns us, on the topic of guidebooks, that "Description is akin to overuse—it destroys; the colors wear off, the corners lose their definition, and in the end what's been described begins to fade, to disappear. This applies most of all to places. [. . .] The truth is terrible: describing is destroying."[11] I will try to avoid this danger as much as possible, hoping that the photographs herein will compensate for a minimum of description.

While most of the photographs included in this volume were taken in Kyoto, a certain number were, while inspired by that city, shot elsewhere. This should not be construed as deception, but rather as a divergent, derivative, differential form of expression. Photography is not only a technique of representation, but also an art of vision. We may indeed speak of the "way of photography" as one speaks of "the way of tea" (*chadō*) or "the way of flowers" (*kadō*). These disciplines not only situate us within a particular culture and teach us how to view the world, but also, however indirectly, they reveal our place in the environment. They are illustrative, in the profound sense of the term. To put this in a Western philosophical perspective, I would cite the famed critic of the spectacle, Guy Debord: "An authentic illustration sheds light on true discourse, like a subordinate clause which is neither incompatible nor pleonastic."[12] A successful photograph constitutes, even when abstract, such an illustration: a non-verbal form of communication indirectly transmitting belief, knowledge, wisdom.

Concerning these images, I would hazard a Zen reference—for Kyoto is *par excellence* the city of Zen—and suggest that a single *kōan* (a paradoxical riddle used in Zen instruction to circumvent the limitations of rationality) might suffice to attain enlightenment, while an entire library might fail. Likewise, the photographs in this book—images of Kyoto as well as images made possible by Kyoto—are not just representations of what one might expect to see in Kyoto, nor documents to illustrate the text, but rather visual epigraphs, oblique allusions, subtle provocations to seek a new vision. They are presented primarily for the pleasure they may offer, in the hope that some may spark a flash of intuition, a secular manifestation of that enlightenment which in Zen is called *satori*.[13]

◆ ◆ ◆

A book can be a great guide, a friend can be an even greater one. A book is occasionally experienced not as a unique and circumscribed entity but rather as an endless process, traversed by friendship. This is why I wish to dedicate this book to those whom I have already thanked for my discovery of Japan: Michaël Ferrier, Michael Lazarin, and Robert Yellin, friends whose erudition concerning this country (and many other things!) is collectively worth an entire library, Baedeker guides included, and whose generosity is inestimable; to Sekitani Kazuhiko and Kawabe Tsutsumi, whose hospitality, benevolence, and insight have been a form of revelation; to my French publisher Anne Bourguignon and my American publisher Peter Goodman, both brilliant editors and passionate Japanophiles; and to Chantal Thomas, extraordinary traveler, whose acute gaze has marvelously accompanied these voyages and this work.

1

Equivocal Thresholds
THE TEA ROOM

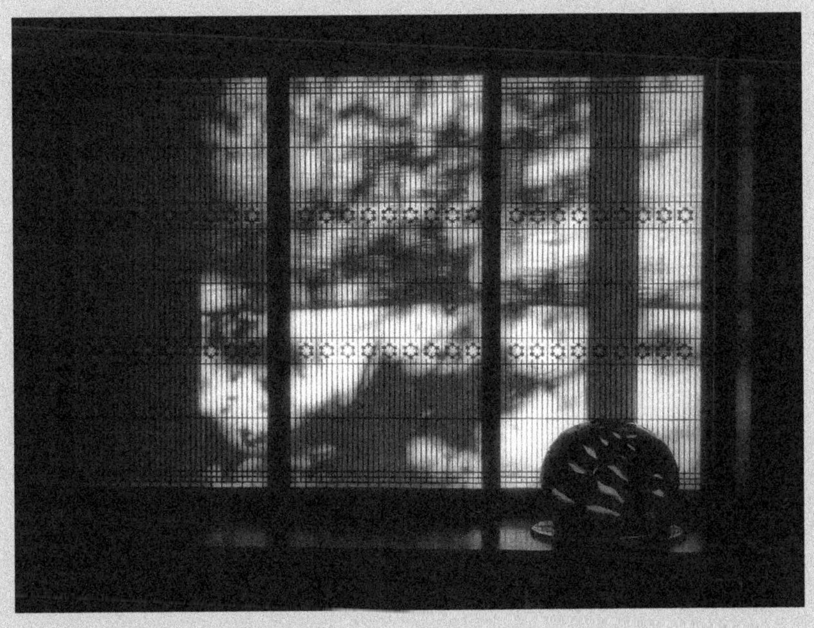

Ryōzanpaku restaurant, Kyoto.

We are symbols and inhabit symbols.
Ralph Waldo Emerson, "Nature"

On 5 December 1933, the Japanese art historian Tsuda Noritake, along with several other dignitaries, attended a tea ceremony at the Odawara estate of Baron Masuda, one of the greatest collectors of Japanese art. This day-long event was dedicated to the appreciation of art according to the protocols of the ceremony, which means that only a very few objects, mostly masterpieces, were chosen according to the seasonal symbolism that guides the ceremony, all harmonized with the aesthetic predilections of the guests. Among the rarities displayed that day was an Ashiyagama iron tea kettle of extraordinary provenance, as its design is said to have been drawn by the great 15th-century painter Sesshū Tōyō (c. 1420–1506), the kettle itself having been used by Takeno Jōō (1502–55), one of the 16th-century founders of the Japanese *wabi-cha*, the tea ceremony based on the aesthetic principles of *wabi* and *sabi* (henceforth abbreviated as wabi-sabi). It is striking that Tsuda chose to begin the introduction to his *History of Japanese Art* (1935), the first major English-language survey of the subject, with the description of this ceremony, a personal anecdote—no less one concerning utilitarian objects—unthinkable for a general survey of Western art.[1] (In comparison, H. W. Janson's *History of Art*, long a standard reference, begins with two Paleolithic parietal cave paintings: the Wounded Bison from Altamira, Spain, and the Black Bull from Lascaux, France, both c. 15,000–10,000 BCE.)[2] Even more astonishing is that this study begins not with painting or sculpture but with a "stone-age" (Mesolithic) Jōmon pottery jar. It will be well to remember that for the

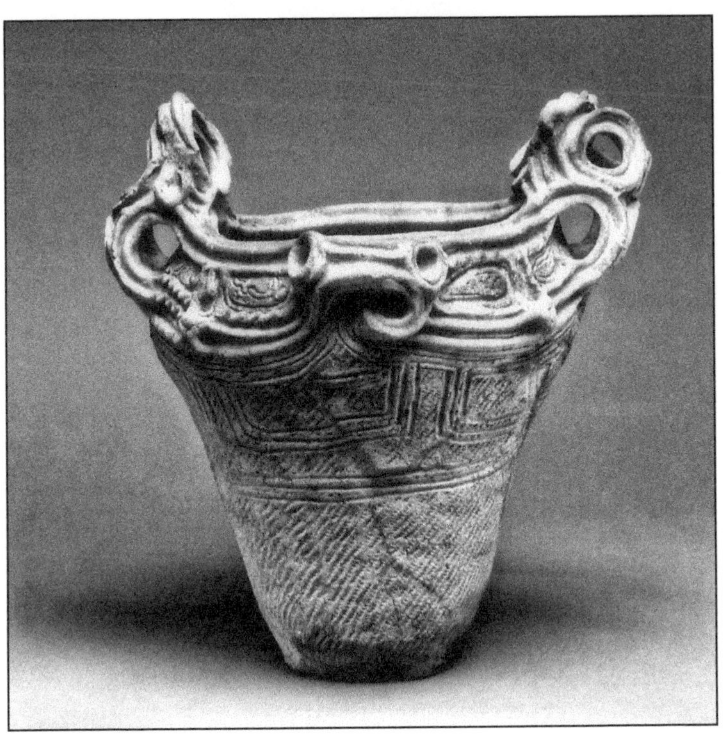

Jōmon ceramic vase, 3500–2500 BCE.

Japanese, this jar emblematizes the very beginnings of their art and culture, suggesting a particular paradigm of art appreciation that shall guide our thoughts.

The tea ceremony (called *chanoyu,* "hot water for tea," or *chadō,* "the way of tea")—a spiritual quest with roots in Zen Buddhism—has inspired a material culture that informs traditional Japanese aesthetics. Its origins are associated with several of the subtemples of the Rinzai Zen temple Daitoku-ji in Kyoto—which remains a major force in contemporary tea culture—and many of the great tea rooms are to be found in Zen temples. It is through objects rather than theology that this culture, this particular form of beauty, this approach to the appreciation of the natural world, this rare form of elegance, this wisdom through beauty, is accessible to the foreigner.

Even if we can't decipher the mysteries, even if we have no chance of enlightenment, we can at least obtain access to a beauty radically different from our own, to discover a trace of the spiritual in the material. One useful summary, however schematic, is that of philosopher Hisamatsu Shin'ichi (1889–1980), who writes of seven characteristics particular to the Zen sensibility: asymmetry, simplicity, austere sublimity, naturalness, subtle profundity or deep reserve, freedom from attachment, tranquility.[3] This configuration of attributes underlies what is referred to as the wabi-sabi aesthetic. Like most broad aesthetic and philosophical terms, both *wabi* and *sabi* are untranslatable by a single word. The challenge of such linguistic difficulties reveals how translation is in fact a way of entering more deeply into a culture, and translating the "untranslatable" occasionally touches upon the most profound realms. (Consider that the very meanings of "truth" and "beauty," even "space" and "time," have been perpetually debated in Western culture ever since the origins of our philosophy in ancient Greece; now try to imagine the difficulty in translating such metaphysical notions into a language that does not contain the equivalent.) Wabi is a state of mind that suggests the positive values of aestheticized poverty and its attendant aspects of tranquility, solitude, humbleness, frugality, asymmetrical harmony, elegant rusticity. Sabi, literally "rust," signifies wear and patination by age and use; it consequently denotes a feeling of familiarity, continuity, history, antiquity, and connotes a corresponding sense of loneliness and sadness (*mono no aware*, the melancholy of the passing of time and the ephemeral nature of things, or as philosopher Michael Lazarin translates, the ecstatic pathos concerning the brevity of beauty).[4] In its extreme instances, sabi suggests bleakness, coldness, desiccation, desolation, extinction.

The tea ceremony, derived from the ethos of monastic Zen experience—a quiet ascetic grace attuned to the beauties and rhythms of nature—reveals that the highest spiritual quest requires the most modest material circumstances. Such is an aestheticized form of detachment from everyday culture, be it bourgeois or courtly. (Of course, the cultural capital constituted by art has always been translated into wealth, power, prestige, and social standing. Since its inception, the idealized intent of chanoyu has been corrupted by the commodity aspect of tea utensils and the utilization of the private space of the tea room for political and financial intrigues. But this hardly obviates its aesthetic and spiritual aspirations.)[5]

There is a famous *kyōgen* (the comic interlude between acts in a Noh play), entitled *Jizō's Dance*, that parodies this ideal in the most hyperbolic manner. It is a sketch about a wandering monk who asks for shelter for the night but is refused because of the interdiction against lodging travelers. However, after repeated pleading, the owner agrees to at least take in the monk's precious straw hat. Soon afterward, the monk appears, as if by magic, under the hat, arguing that as long as he stays beneath the hat, it is the hat that is sheltering him, and not the house, so no law is broken. The owner, amused, agrees to the arrangement, and in repayment for his kindness, the monk does a dance, which is the finale of the piece.[6] In his classic 12th-century memoir, *Hōjōki* (1212; The Ten Foot Square Hut), one of the greatest Zen-inspired

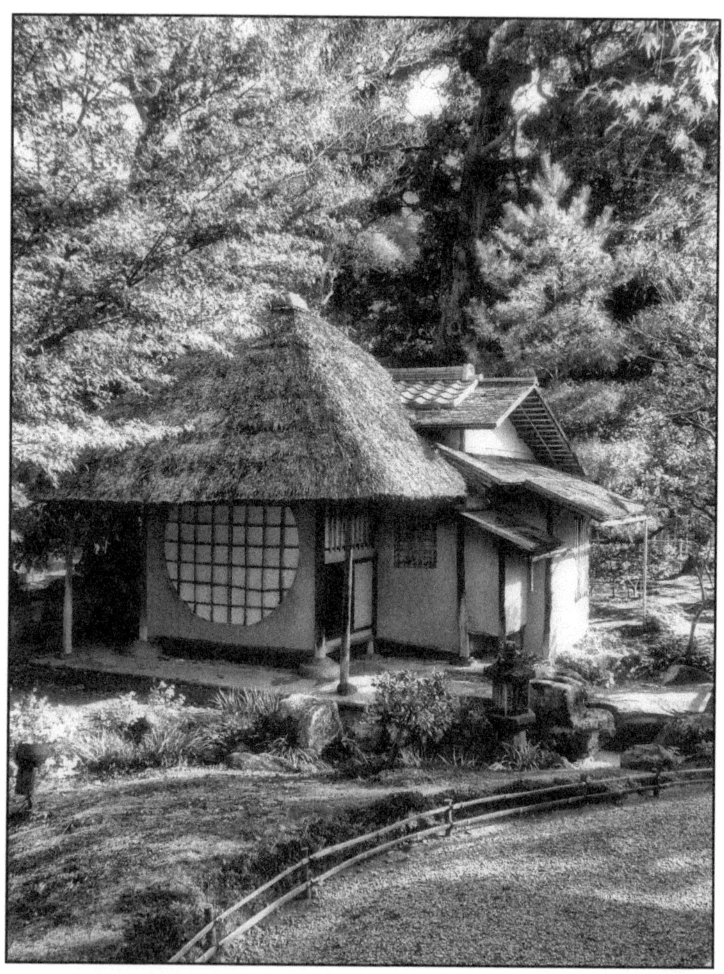

Tea pavilion, Kōdai-ji.

literary works, Kamo no Chōmei (1155–1216) expresses a sentiment common to Japanese poetry and drama: "Where to find a place to rest for a while? And how bring even short-lived peace to our hearts?"[7]

The architecture emblematic of this aesthetic is the Japanese tea hut, among the most refined and most private of edifices. Yet its ideal is of the simplest, on the border between architecture and bricolage. *Hōjōki* is a major precursor to this sensibility. Its author, Kamo no Chōmei, was a minor court poet and member of a family of Shinto priests serving the Shimogamo shrine, but since he didn't receive an expected appointment to this sanctuary, he converted to Zen Buddhism. When Kamo no Chōmei claims that "people in the world do not build houses to suit their real needs,"[8] he is of course referring to their spiritual and aesthetic needs, which is why in shifting from a worldly to a literary and spiritual existence he first moved into a house a tenth the size of his former one (the newer house perhaps being comparable, *mutatis mutandis*, to Shisen-dō, the great scholar Ishikawa Jōzan's home in the eastern hills of Kyoto),[9] and finally into the celebrated forest hut, one hundredth its size.

This retreat to a tiny hut in the mountains to the southeast of Kyoto—in order to escape the catastrophes ravaging Kyoto and enjoy the passing seasons while practicing his poetry in peace and quiet—became legendary.[10] *Hōjōki* is simultaneously a lament for the impermanence caused by human and natural catastrophes and a celebration of the melancholic beauty that results from the transience (*mujō*) of the natural world. That this revelation takes place in the most fragile of abodes is only fitting. This is the shelter of lore—contemporaneous with the mountain huts of ascetics and literati as depicted in the Chinese Southern Song Dynasty (1127–1279) paintings so beloved by the Japanese—a sort of informal hermitage where the traveler can spend a single night, where there is little distinction between inside and outside, and where the ephemera of nature are at one with the extreme flimsiness of the abode, as well as of its occupant: "... we and our houses fleeting, hollow ..."[11] Ultimately, the author feels that he cannot sufficiently detach himself from the world to attain enlightenment, not only because of the pleasure he takes in the beauty of the seasons, but also because "the way I love this hut is itself an attachment."[12] He thus espouses, with no little psychological torment, the worldly, rather than the strictly spiritual, side of Buddhism, which is precisely why he abandoned the monastic life in the first place. Kamo no Chōmei lived the consequences of authentic, profound austerity to the fullest, practicing a deeply aesthetic asceticism.

Kamo no Chōmei's hut is one of the precursors of the wabi-sabi tea pavilion. The tea hut or pavilion is more a state of mind than a work of architecture, the simulacrum of rustic austerity rather than its reality. It is both the most specialized and the most idealized environment, where space is condensed, time distended, attention focused. It exists for but a sole purpose: drinking a well-prepared bowl of tea. But what a preparation! One examines the objects *in*, but not the construction *of*, a tea room. The conceit central to the Japanese tea ceremony was stated by the greatest of all tea masters, Sen no Rikyū (1522–91), who perfected its wabi-sabi version that perdures to this day: the tea ceremony is nothing but *chanoyu*, "hot water for tea." While the wabi-sabi aesthetic ideal subtends the aesthetics suggested by huts inspired by that of Kamo no Chōmei, the architectural reality is quite different. Even the most cursory consideration of a tea ceremony reveals the internal contradictions of this aestheticized "poverty": the "simplicity" of properly serving a cup of tea takes place according to a precisely choreographed ritual following the most rigorous etiquette (only

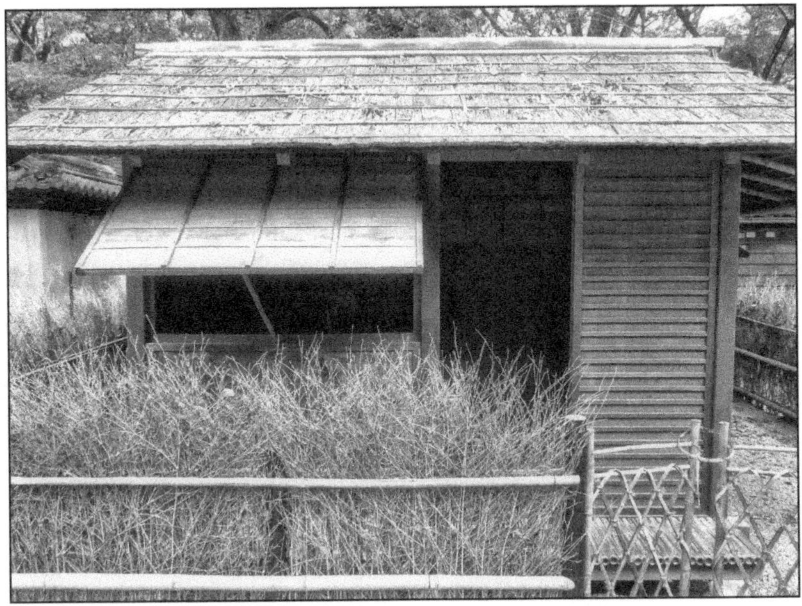

Kamo no Chōmei's hut (modern reconstruction at Kawai-jinja).

fully mastered after years of study and practice), which in its full form lasts several hours; the "humble" vessels used to make and serve the tea may be treasures of inestimable value; and the tiny "impoverished" hut in which it takes place costs more per square meter than the magnificent villa that sits alongside it. The reality of these material contradictions contains a myth, an ideal, a utopia.

The formalized gestures of the ceremony—etiquette considered as "proper form" (*reishiki*)—constitute an integral part of what Okakura Kakuzō (1863–1913), in *The Book of Tea*, writes of as a "moral geometry," one that guarantees one's harmonious place in a particular space, community, and in the universe as a whole.[13] To imagine that all architectural geometry is fundamentally moral geometry is to

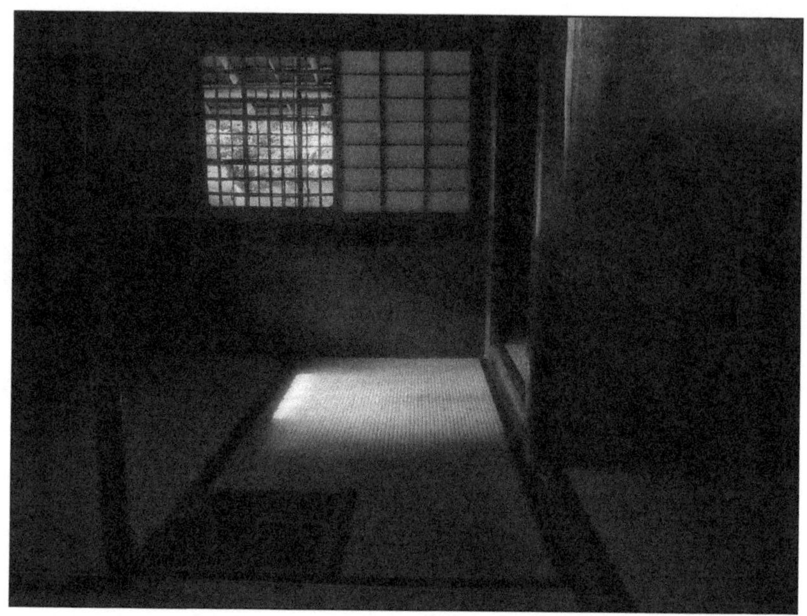

Tea room, Kōtō-in.

approach the exemplary ethical and metaphysical sense of the tea room. The tea room or pavilion is meaningless outside the context of the ceremony. (However, I must admit, from an outsider's perspective, that many of them would make the perfect writer's cabin, though to my knowledge this is never done.) True to the spirit of Zen, it is essentially a void given clarity by our acts. Okakura writes of the tea room as an "Abode of Vacancy": "The tea-room is absolutely empty, except for what may be placed there temporarily to satisfy some aesthetic mood."[14] This mood, attuned to the seasons, is conveyed by the choice of tea utensils, the theme of the drawing or calligraphy placed in the display alcove (*tokonoma*), and a flower arrangement (*chabana*) of the simplest sort.

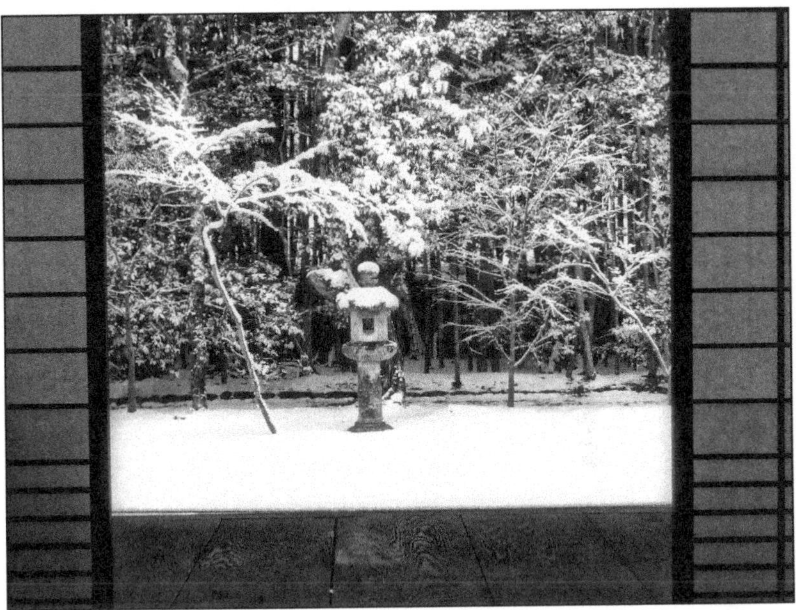

Kōtō-in.

The novelist Tanizaki Jun'ichirō, in his extraordinary *In Praise of Shadows*, goes even further, claiming that ". . . the beauty of a Japanese room depends on a variation of shadows, heavy shadows against light shadows—it has nothing else."[15] The entirety of the tea room design is conceived in support of shadows: very little light is admitted by the rice-paper-covered windows (*shōji*), and the light that enters by the transom or emanates from lamps is carefully directed to subtly illuminate the objects and guests. Colors are carefully chosen, for in addition to the sundry shades of black and white that derive from ink drawings, as A. L . Sadler notes, "in decoration their most favored hues are Ash color, Tea color and Mouse color."[16] According to Tanizaki, these colors are chosen expressly to make the light practically

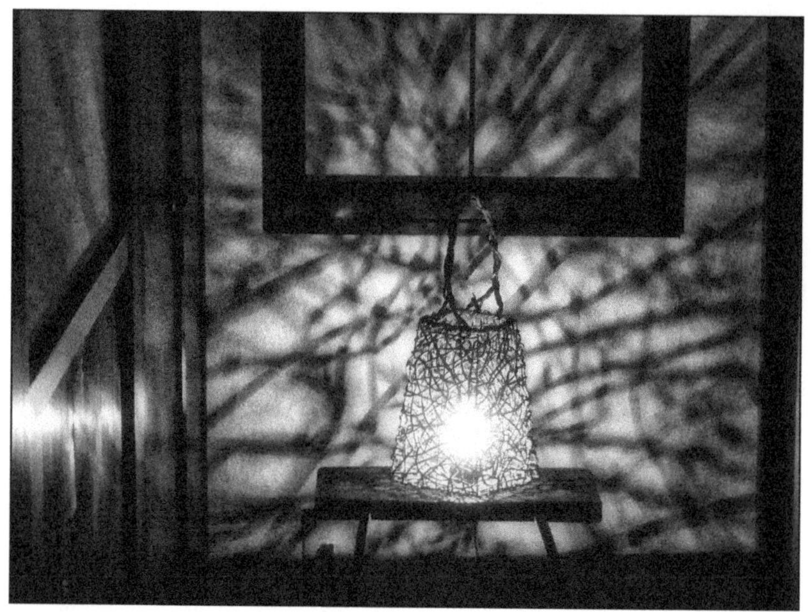

Shadows at the Oyado Tanaka inn, Wajima.

disappear, and artificial lighting, when such there is, remains extremely discreet: "We do our walls in neutral colors so that the sad, fragile, dying rays can sink into absolute repose,"[17] such that, "the scroll and the flowers serve not as ornament but rather to give depth to the shadows."[18] The object as repoussoir of the void.

In fact, light and shadow constitute the very basis of Japanese chanoyu design principles, a veritably immaterial architectural foundation. Tanizaki: "We delight in the mere sight of the delicate glow of fading rays clinging to the surface of a dusky wall, there to live out what little life remains to them. We never tire of the sight, for to us this pale glow and these dim shadows far surpass any ornament."[19] I remember a tea ceremony that took place at the Injō-ji temple (Senbon Emma-dō) early one New Year's Eve. All was ready, the lighting was subdued to perfection, the shadows beautifully articulated the ritual space, when suddenly the guest of honor—obviously not a tea aficionado—looked up toward the ceiling and said that he couldn't see clearly, and out of deference the tea master turned up the lights. The spell was broken, and what ensued felt more like a demonstration than a ceremony. One can't but remember what Tanizaki writes of the tokonoma: "Were the shadows to be banished from its corners, the alcove would in that instant revert to mere void."[20] We were confronted by a banal reality—the incorrect postures of the guests, motley and indecorous clothes, awkward gestures, inappropriate comments—precisely what we had entered the tea room to escape.

Wabi-cha (the tea ceremony practiced according to wabi-sabi aesthetics) is a state of mind and a way of life, yet when reduced to its material forms, ritualistic elements and pure connoisseurship, it becomes mannerist, even decadent. The spiritual gives way to the purely material. As photographer and artist Okamoto Tarō (1911–96)—whose photos would later greatly inspire me at the MoMA exhibition to be discussed in the next chapter—explains, when esoteric aesthetic knowledge is passed on through secret transmission, and material wealth is a precondition for obligatory initiation rites, "connoisseurship came to seek out not the intense outpouring of vitality, but rather its minute intricacies. Art became degraded to a world of fashion, flavor and form."[21] Such is the risk of abandoning the spiritual for the material: one might say that this is true for every aesthetic system in the world.

Thus the tea hut is ideally more a site of aesthetic vision

and spiritual sensibility than an architectural structure *per se*. The Modernist roots—according to which architect and architectural theorist Adolf Loos considered decoration tantamount to a crime—of architect Bruno Taut (1880–1938) had prepared him for the pure lines, undecorated surfaces, neutral colors, and empty spaces of traditional Japanese design. In writing that would inspire generations of architects in both Europe and Japan, he offered what may be the best definition of the tea hut: "This is not architecture, but improvised lyricism."[22] Similarly, decades earlier, Okakura had already called the tea room an "Abode of Fancy"—ephemeral and not intended for posterity—since each one is specifically designed according to a particular tea master's aesthetic vision.[23] However, this hasn't prevented the great tea huts and rooms from being preserved and cherished above all other domestic structures in Japan.

These spaces cannot be reduced to mathematical formulas, as can most Western buildings; these rooms are more akin to craft than to design or architecture. Their interiors are almost impossible to adequately describe in detail, both because they only come alive in their use and because of their artisanal material complexity: they are constructed of a wide variety of woods in either their raw, weathered, or hand-worked states (a traditional tea room is constructed of eighteen different types of wood, of varying degrees of rarity); of different sorts of hand-made papers for both window panes and wall coverings; of plaster in varying neutral tones without standardized hues. And they are finished by laying hand-made *tatami* (floor mats).

A small range of materials, an enormous depth of detail. The tea room is the inseparable background to the ceremony and its objects, and when closely examined, it—like the tea utensils exhibited within—admits of the general principles of craft appreciation that guide any examination of hand-made objects, as theorist and woodworker David Pye explains: "As the observer approaches the object, new elements, previously indistinguishable, successively appear and come into play aesthetically. Equally, and inevitably, the larger elements drop out and become ineffective as you approach. But new incidents appear at every step until finally your eye gets too close to be focused."[24] And of course, the objects in question being utilitarian craft, the sense of touch takes over at the very point where visual focus becomes impossible.

Yet the tea room is not intended to be admired as a construction, nor even to be seen in all its details, not least of all due to the play of shadows. Rather, it creates an ambiance, an atmosphere, to serve the spiritual and aesthetic purposes of the ceremony. Its role is not to be visible, but to render visible—in part by the play of shadow, as Tanizaki insists—accentuating both the *exhibition* of the tea objects and the *performance* of the tea ceremony. The sense of isolation, quietude, and intimacy all foster an acute and extended concentration on objects, gestures, and the conversation that ensues: a hyperbolic paradigm of aesthetic absorption. The objects are few: on the mat between the host and guests are those utensils necessary for making tea, notably the tea bowl (*chawan*), which is near the summit of the aesthetic hierarchy in Japan; in the tokonoma will be placed a painted or calligraphic scroll, often a precious ceramic object, and a simple bouquet (chabana), all chosen according to a seasonal theme. The ceremony is lengthy, and the most formal ones may last for hours, including not only the making of thick and thin tea, but also a full *kaiseki* meal. The appreciation is intense: objects are chosen according to the guests' levels of discrimination, and appropriate commentary is part of the ritual.[25]

The tea room is a work of art, a statement of taste, a site of performance, a space of exhibition, a setting for commensality, an idealized shelter, an extended metaphor, and a state of mind. It is a utopia that guides our vision, our sensibility, our taste, but like all utopias it needs to be perpetually reimagined, otherwise it quickly becomes obsolete, or turns dystopian.[26] Even if one cannot manage the required ritualized gestures or adopt the decorous ceremonial attitude, even if linguistic incapacity does not permit the appropriate form of participation, a heightened state of mindfulness and solicitude is a form of grace available to all. For a traveler in quest of utopias, what is essential is not the belief that they may exist, but rather that the very thought of one will inform every other space, for in the imagination is the preservation of the world.

2

Other Modernities
THE MUSEUM

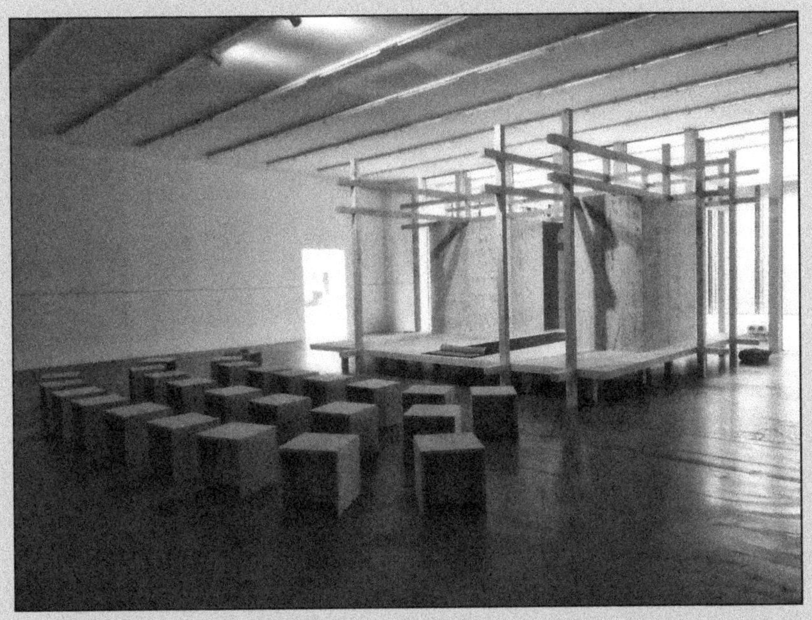

Tea pavilion, Aargauer Kunsthaus.

The tea room haunts domestic space, and since the ceremony is hyperbolically situational, the tea aesthetic is infinitely malleable. It is a given in Japan that, despite its utilitarian function, the tea bowl—and by extension, ceramics in general—is what in the West would be referred to as a "work of art," and the tea ceremony is the art form that contains all other art forms, a sort of proto-Gesamtkunstwerk. This total work of art also takes another form in Japan: the restaurant. It is often said that the first contact with a culture—usually well before traveling to the country in question—is through its cuisine, and regarding Japan this necessarily means exposure to fine ceramics. It is fundamentally impossible to dissociate cuisine, ceramics, architecture, flower arranging, and so forth in Japan, where a traditional art form is rarely experienced on its own. While it is often the case in Japanese restaurants outside of Japan that the ceramic dishes and sake cups are quite attractive, one is hardly prepared for the experience of dining in Japan, where the tableware in upscale restaurants often consists of creations by famed contemporary potters and where it is not unheard of to eat and drink from works by Living National Treasures or from rare antique vessels. For in relation to ceramics, we must remember that there is a vast schism between their appreciation in the West, where pottery is still generally relegated to the realm of "craft," and in Japan, where pottery has long existed among the highest forms of art.[1]

Ceramics provide the focus of the Japanese tea ceremony—in the broad context of calligraphy, painting, flower arranging, architecture, gardens, textiles, lacquer, metalwork, cuisine—and the ceremony in turn establishes the aesthetic paradigms at the core of traditional Japanese culture, still very much alive. Integral to the ceremony is kaiseki, what initially began as the simple cuisine of cha-noyu—three dishes and a soup, meticulously prepared but presented in total simplicity—and eventually evolved into the refined haute cuisine first of Kyoto, then of all Japan. As is the case in the tea ceremony, the choice of pottery for each course depends upon the visual qualities of the food being served, the season with all of its poetic allusions, the weather with its subtle atmospheric ambiance, and the desire to accord with the aesthetic acumen of the guests. In short, the choice of ceramics in both everyday life and in the rarified world of the tea ceremony is of great complexity. In what follows, it should be remembered that ceramics provide the vessels for both food and flowers, both in the tea room and the restaurant.

Composer and artist Christian Marclay recounts the following anecdote. One day photographer, architect, and collector Sugimoto Hiroshi organized a ceremony in the Imameido tea room of his Manhattan studio, in which he hung one of Marclay's works, from a series of brightly colored scrolls depicting explosions and the onomatopoeia of catastrophic sounds derived from manga and graphic novels, mounted like a traditional *kakejiku* (hanging scroll with elaborate silk borders) created by a master craftsman in Tokyo.[2] In the tokonoma was a small, round ceramic vase with a simple chabana flower arrangement. As Marclay examined the vase, Sugimoto explained that in fact it was a hand grenade from the Second World War! (When Japan ran out of metal as the war progressed, they manufactured ceramic grenades.) Such is a brilliant example of *mitate mono*, the Japanese version of repurposing, in the context of tea.

An object or ritual that enters the museum is radically transformed. In 2015 the Aargauer Kunsthaus in Aarau, Switzerland, organized an exhibition of paintings by Marclay that included works from the above-mentioned series. The exhibition also included a highly stylized and particularly untraditional tea pavilion in which some of the scrolls were displayed. More a well-lit theatrical space than a tea room, dozens of chairs set up in front effectively turned it into a stage, the site of what was to be a tea ceremony performed by the Zurich-based tea master Mukai Yumi. However, Mukai realized that the exhibition conditions made it impossible to do a proper ceremony: the design of the tea hut was inappropriate, an open platform rather than a closed space; the lighting was harsh and direct, without shadow; not only were the materials not "noble," but one could still smell the scent of the newly cut wood, rendering the environment totally without sabi; and those invited were spectators rather than participants, fixed in their chairs at a distance from the stage. The performance conditions suggested more a demonstration than a ceremony. Since a traditional chanoyu was impossible, she decided to create what amounted to the simulacrum of a tea ceremony, going through the gestures appropriate to the edicts of her tea school (Urasenke), but without using any water! Following this unorthodox, indeed eccentric if not outlandish, variant of a tea ceremony, the space was indeed transformed into a stage when the curator Madeleine Schuppli and I joined Mukai for a discussion.

I was initially at a loss for words following this fascinating aberration of a tea ceremony, however intriguing

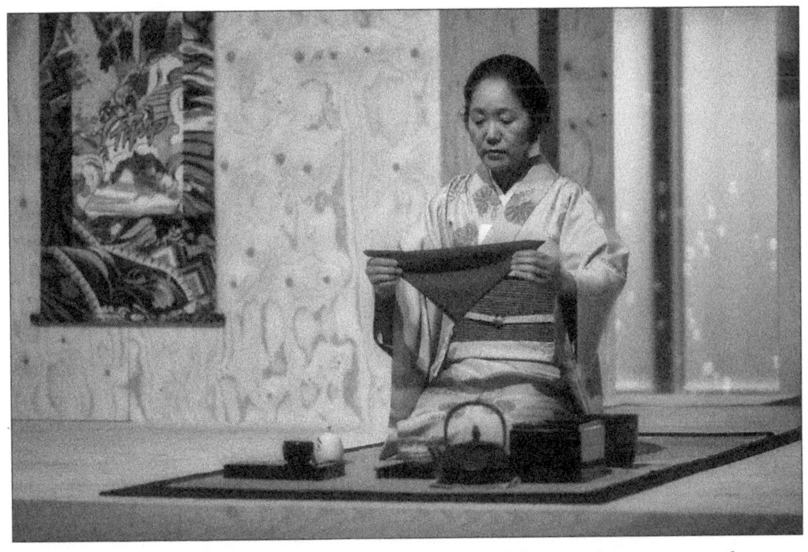

Tea performance by Mukai Yumi as part of the exhibition Christian Marclay:
Action *at the Aargauer Kunsthaus, 30 August – 15 November 2015.*

it might have been, having no idea how to relate Marclay's
scrolls to the performance. My attention wandering, I did
what one normally does in such circumstances after the tea
is shared: I contemplated the chawan used in the ceremony.
And suddenly I understood: the ancient tea bowl had at
one point been damaged and consequently repaired by the
traditional *kintsugi* technique—where transparent lacquer
filled with gold dust is used to make the repair—accentuating rather than dissimulating the crack. The damaged tea
bowl echoed the scenes of destruction in the scrolls! Afterward, Mukai Yumi suggested a parallel between the violence
of Marclay's paintings and her performance: "I was in the
background of my performance and was not a person who
made a performance, I was a material. I hoped the guests saw
only red silk moving, not me or my hands, and heard the

crush and scream of the bowl. So red of silk was like blood of tea bowl."[3]

Antithetical aesthetics

In its ideal instance, the tea room is a place of total concentration, a retreat without distraction, a utopia with a single ritualistic purpose, a space that prepares one for enlightenment. The Western museum was conceived for a very different, but equally profound, sort of meditation, in part derived from the veneration of devotional objects and images in the sacred space of the church. However, the museum has devolved into a site of almost total distraction, where the lengthy, unimpeded contemplation of art is all but impossible, to the point where in many museums even benches have been eliminated so as to improve crowd flow and hasten departure.

But even in the best of circumstances, serious viewing of art objects in the West follows different habits and protocols from those in Japan, and each type of art makes different demands on the viewer. So it is imperative to contrast the intimate, secret, shadowy, heterogeneous space of the tea room with the public, panoptical, bright, homogeneous space of the white cube of the art gallery or museum, so well described by Brian O'Doherty's *Inside the White Cube*: "Unshadowed, white, clean, artificial—the space is devoted to the technology of esthetics."[4] Remembering Tanizaki's claim that "were the shadows to be banished from its corners, the alcove would in that instant revert to mere void,"[5] it is apparent that the tenebrous invisibility of tea architecture permits the tenuous visibility of the object, leaving as much room for imagination as for vision. In the tea room, objects are incidents of vision, articulations of time and space, instigators of gestures, motivations for social relations. It is the ambiance, not just the architecture and design, that creates the context.

One must remain sensitive to the different poles of aesthetic discourse, roughly schematized as the difference between amateur and professional appreciation, and further differentiated by the diverse exigencies of private and public viewing. In *Distinction: A Social Critique of the Judgment of Taste*, Pierre Bourdieu distinguishes the two fundamental modes of aesthetic discourse in contemporary Western cultures as either that typical of people who grew up in homes filled with art (the attitude of the connoisseur) or that characteristic of those who encountered art in museums and schools (exemplified by the specialist).[6]

In Japan, museum culture was mainly an offshoot of American influence, beginning in the 19th century during the Meiji period, then in an accelerated manner after the Second World War. To the contrary, centuries of art appreciation in Japan—in the context of tea culture—took place in the form of the most intimate (though hardly rigorous or scientific) connoisseurship. Many vestiges of this private and comparatively secret aesthetic culture obtain today, thus complicating the task of the outsider who wishes to gain knowledge of this world.[7]

The public museum tends to extricate art from the environment, abstracting it into an ideal world with extremely limited viewing possibilities, where the background colors, sight lines, viewing distances, and much else tend to be invariable, all meant to bring the art work into a collective albeit ideal space, to ultimately present the work as an autonomous object, or even a world unto itself. In contrast, the private collection, especially when gathered in a home, tends to integrate the art work into the rest of the personal—and often idiosyncratic or downright eccentric—environment, essentially transforming art into part of the decor. Such is not necessarily a bad thing, as is often suggested in a quite derogatory manner by Western art critics. This is *a fortiori* the case for functional works such as tea bowls, which for many in the West would not even rise to the level of "decor," much less art.

While this decorative proclivity should not necessarily imply a disparagement of the art work, it is usually approached in a critical manner, since decor serves a purpose, and until recently most modernist Western art critics wrote under the influence of Immanuel Kant's characterization of art as "purposeful purposelessness." The appropriateness of certain idiosyncratic conditions of private display may be debatable, but tailoring the viewing situation to one's own preferences offers undisputable advantages: lengthy viewing in calm, quiet, comfortable, uncrowded circumstances—perhaps even with wine, whisky, or sake in hand—is certainly preferable to battling crowds in a museum. While these private aesthetic environments are created in the West on an *ad hoc* basis, usually in accord with the ephemeral vagaries of taste and style, in Japan a half millennium of tea aesthetics is there to guide the art aficionado in establishing an appropriate decor.[8]

To illuminate the tea room is to annul the realm of the ceremony and enter the history of its architecture. We might contrast a very different void from a radically different context, Yves Klein's infamous 1958 exhibition *Le vide* (The Void), where he presented the empty Iris Clert Gallery in Paris as a work of art. By purging the space of any art works, the focus was on the well-illuminated gallery itself, which was transformed into—as in a Gestalt figure/ground switch—an aestheticized object. Since the avant-garde of the 1950s through the 1970s was increasingly concerned with the conceptualization, dematerialization, and decommodification of the art object, the traditional art milieu became—through a determined critique of social order, finance, and power—the object of art itself, with the gallery as the last material stage that separated object from concept. Vacate and illuminate the white cube, and art is brought to a new dialectical level; vacate and illuminate the tea room, and one finds but an empty space awaiting dusting.

At one extreme, traditional chanoyu may be stifled by the sclerotic mannerism that often occurs in the guise of preserving tradition; at the other, it may suffer from the self-destructive iconoclasm of an avant-garde that values change for change's sake. There is a fundamental paradox to the aesthetics of the tea ceremony. Each great tea master evolves a particular style, which includes the design of the tea room and the choice of utensils. Such ensembles primarily have meaning in relation to the style of that particular master; once he is gone, a new style under a new master should evolve, as when Rikyū's austere wabi-cha—which we need remember was, in his time, revolutionary—was superseded by the often extravagant, some would even say mannerist or decadent, style of his acolyte Furuta Oribe (1544–1615).

Just like the most radical works of the Western avant-garde, the once innovative and often astonishing objects and gestures of the tea ceremony are preserved over time to be eventually integrated into art history and end up in museums. Such a process results in what we call tradition. It is essential, then, to put things in their historical perspective.

Common belief has it that Rikyū created the purest form of the traditional tea ceremony, but in fact his tea style was a true avant-garde, in the literal sense of the word, since it was created for the militarist ruler Hideyoshi Toyotomi (who unified Japan by the sword). This resulted in a tea ceremony more in the spirit of military rigor and austerity than courtly luxury and frivolousness. This also explains its affiliation with Zen Buddhism, which was taken up by the warlords as a religion based on action rather than scripture.

It is a commonplace to claim that wars bring technological advances; they also often effect aesthetic transformations. Following Rikyū's death during the years of the unification of Japan, the Edo period (1603–1868) brought over two hundred and fifty years of continual peace in a highly controlled, authoritarian environment. During that time, when individual initiative and innovation was frowned upon, the slow perfecting of traditional forms— rather than radical innovation—became the norm. This led to the way of tea becaming a conservative tradition, with its precepts and precious objects passed down through family and temple lineage across the generations, establishing a codification of beauty that in some instances turned to mannerism and at others to sheer repetition and superficiality. But we must not forget that chanoyu began as an aesthetic revolution, one that has been revived in our times. The path from the traditional wabi-sabi tea ceremony to contemporary avant-garde manifestations led from a nearly architectureless ambiance to the ostentation of high design, from shadowy mystery to brilliant ostentation, from austere yet elegant rusticity to urban post-modern hybridity. One designs for one's gestures and one's times; reciprocally, the traditional tea room inflects contemporary vision and

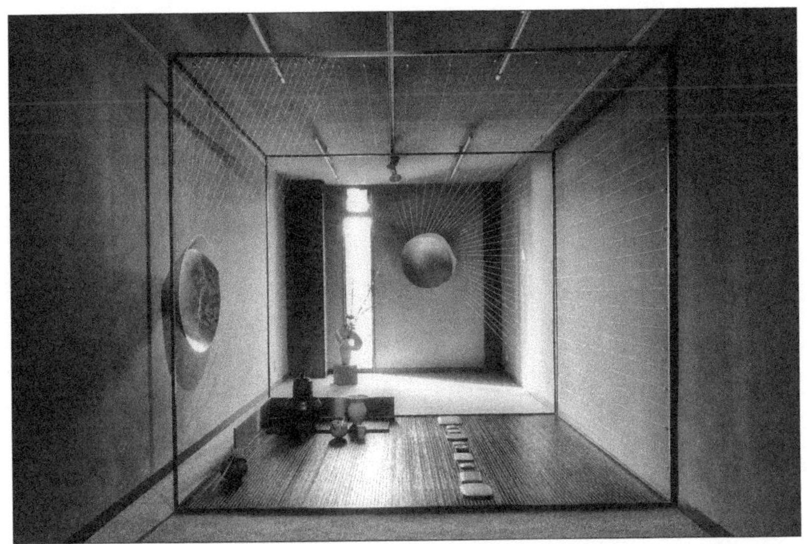

Tea room by Fukumoto Fuku at the Utsuwakan Gallery, Kyoto.

modulates current gestures. What may be claimed for the tea room is generally true of all architecture: it is the lived space, not the empty shell, that counts.

◆ ◆ ◆

I would like to ask if the reader could name three living potters. Or maybe just one. Knowing the difficulty in doing this—so far nobody I have asked outside of Japan, other than some potters and collectors, has obliged—I will give the reader another chance and simply ask for the name of a single great potter, living or dead. In most cases the answer comes back as "Picasso," who indeed created fabulous ceramics but who could hardly be classified by the single term "potter." Miro is a close second, though disqualified for the same reason. Lucio Fontana would be a much better response, though few realize that he was fundamentally a

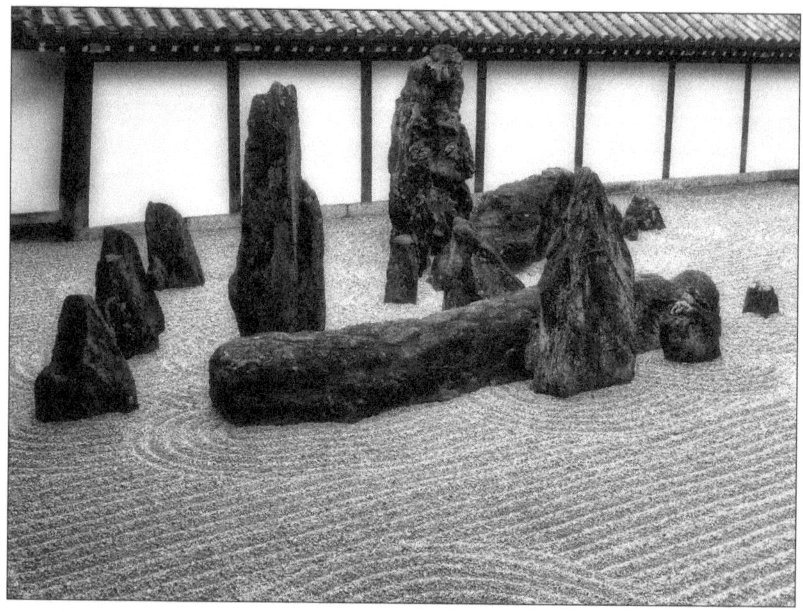

Tōfuku-ji.

ceramic artist. Given my recent research, collecting, and writing, needless to say I can provide an answer, and it was thus with great anticipation that in January 2013 I entered the exhibition *Tokyo 1955–1970: A New Avant Garde* at the Museum of Modern Art in New York. I had already begun writing what would become *The Grain of the Clay: Reflections on Ceramics and the Art of Collecting* (2016), an ode to contemporary Japanese pottery, and I was obviously full of expectations about what I would discover in this museum that has informed my appreciation of art since my youth. I was well aware that a show on the Japanese postwar avant-garde would not deal with either utilitarian ceramics or traditional art (despite the extent to which such works might serve as appropriate foils for some of the pieces displayed),

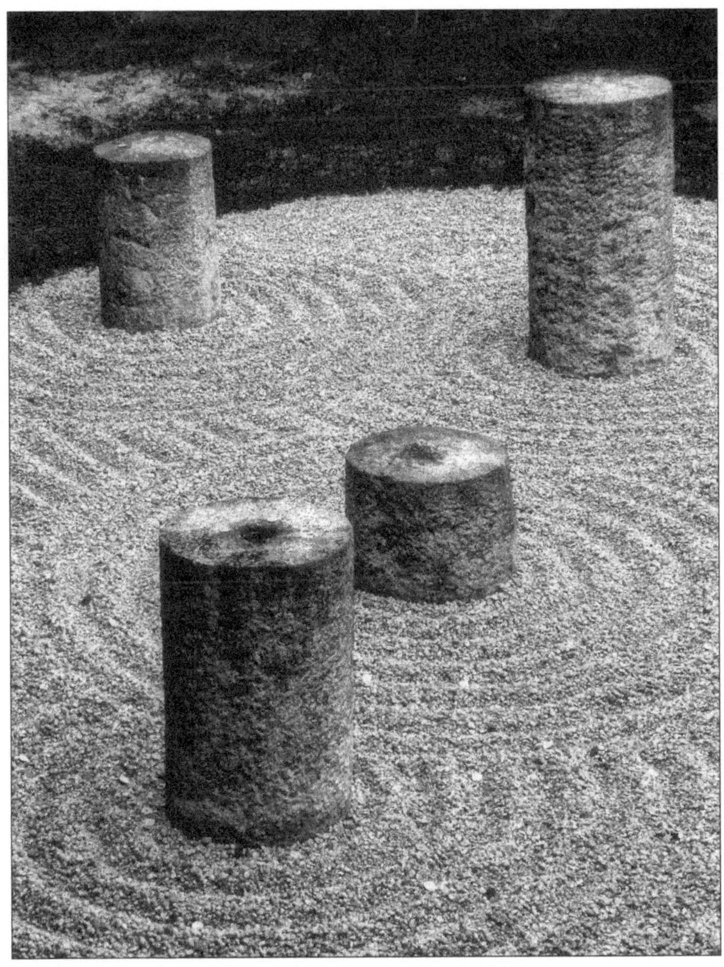

Tōfuku-ji.

but I was absolutely certain that the modernist legacy of ceramics and flower arranging—two art forms that are inextricably intertwined—in Japan would be represented. My hopes were founded on a confluence of factors. Many

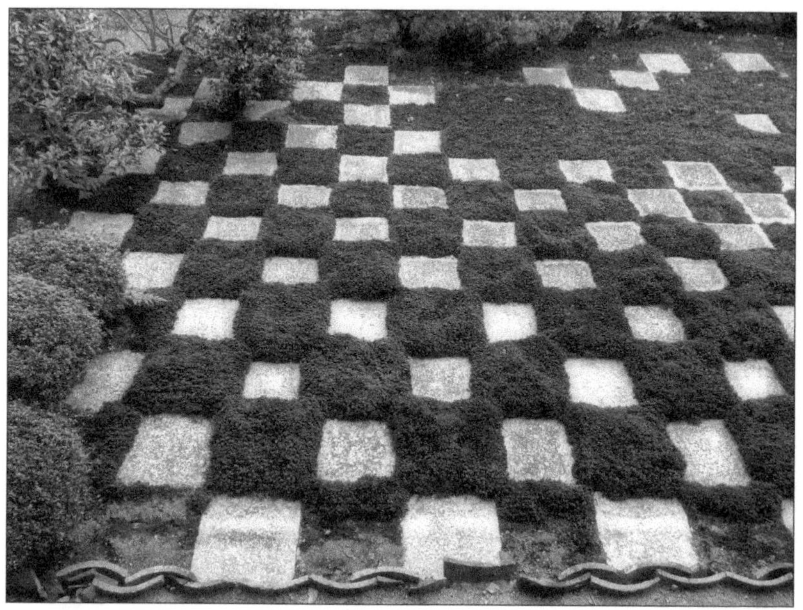

Tōfuku-ji.

important developments of Japanese modernism may be traced back to the association in the 1930s—yet to be adequately researched in the West—between Teshigahara Sōfū (1900–1979), founder of the Sōgetsu *ikebana* school, and the ikebana and garden specialist Shigemori Mirei (1896–1975), destined to become the preeminent postwar Japanese landscape architect, beginning with the gardens, among the most admired in Japan, that he created at the Kyoto temple Tōfuku-ji in 1939.[9]

It was with the fabulous creative effervescence and the tangle of artistic relations of this period in mind—an extraordinary moment for both ceramics and sculpture—that I entered the *Tokyo 1955-1970* exhibition at MoMA, and I bounded with joy to see the first works on display:

two photographs from 1956 by Okamoto Tarō, depicting an earthenware vessel and an earthenware figurine both from the Jōmon period.[10] The choice and juxtaposition of the subject matter were particularly felicitous: that the show began with ceramic works revealed great sensitivity to Japanese culture; that one was functional and the other sculptural established the opposition at the core of the potter's creative dilemma in the postwar years; that the works were Jōmon, the very origins of Japanese art, suggested a culture-specific symbolism.[11] The earliest periods of Japanese culture are distinguished as Jōmon and Yayoi, roughly akin to the European Mesolithic (middle stone age) and Neolithic (late stone age) periods, each of which correspond to typical—one might well say archetypical—forms of ceramic art. Some Japanese cultural critics have gone so far as to suggest that the difference between Jōmon and Yayoi represents the two fundamental polarities of the Japanese soul, not unlike Friedrich Nietzsche's distinction between the Dionysian and the Apollonian. One could well imagine the entire exhibition articulated according to this dichotomy.

Furthermore, selecting Okamoto Tarō to begin the exhibition was an inspired choice, given that he spent part of the 1930s in Paris, studying at the Sorbonne and associating with Picasso, Breton, and the other Surrealists, thus receiving his aesthetic education at the fount of European Modernism. Yet he too was divided between cultures, styles, and epochs, for along with his avant-garde tendencies he would also subsequently publish books on the most traditional Japanese arts, such as *Rediscovery of the Japan—Topography of Art* (1958) and *Mysteries in Japan* (1964), both of which were inspired by his passion for Jōmon pottery.[12] What might appear to be a contradiction—the simultaneous passion for the most avant-garde and the most traditional work—is in fact at the core of modernism in Japan, where there is often an alternation between, and occasionally a syncretism of, traditionalism and westernization. It is precisely this sort of boundary crossing that amplifies the complexities of travel and cultural exchange. In short, this was surely the exhibition I awaited.

As I viewed the exhibit, totally engrossed by many unexpected discoveries, I temporarily forgot my fundamental reason for being there, but as I progressed I felt a growing disappointment. No flower arrangements, no tea ceremony, *no ceramics*. Finally, I understood: the two Okamoto Tarō photographs were in fact included not as representations of pottery but as graphic art! My initial excitement was due to a serious category error: I had confused signifier and signified! On exhibit were, of course, photographs, not pottery!

◆ ◆ ◆

One of the most beautiful lessons of the Buddha is the "Flower Sermon." Gathered around him, his disciples await words of wisdom. After a certain moment of silence, he simply raises in his hand a white lotus. That gesture, with its symbolic flower, constitutes the sermon. Might we conclude that every self-reflective gesture is a sermon of sorts, and every flower, indeed every object, a symbol? I would suggest that we pause to absorb the beauty of this lesson, and also remember that reading includes the pauses we take for reflection. Few offerings can be as aesthetically and symbolically perfect as the Buddha's lotus, but can the real ever be as pure as the ideal, the object as perfect as the symbol? Has any bouquet placed on the altar of a Buddhist temple, however splendid, matched the perfection of that

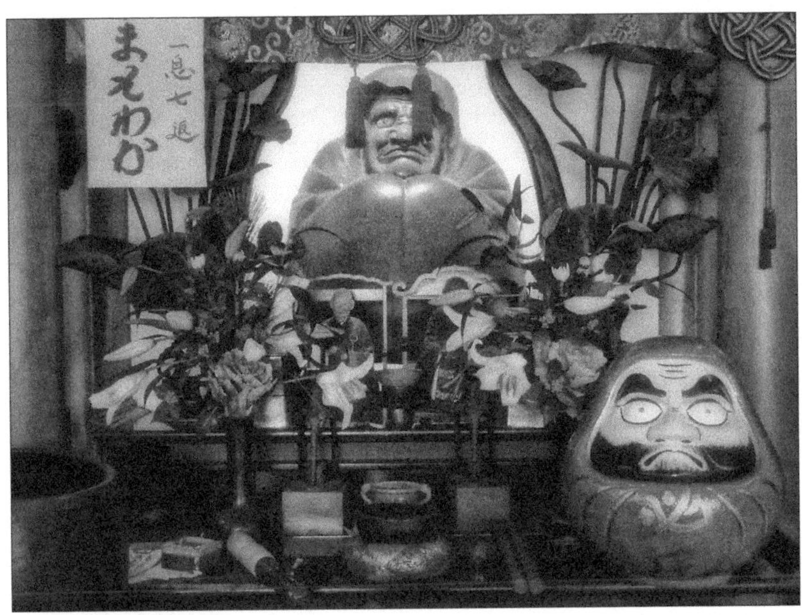

Altar, Daruma-dera.

originary lotus? One can understand why the most perfect specimens should be saved for the gods, so why waste them on mortals, especially in Japan, where the wabi-sabi aesthetic valorizes imperfections of all sorts, especially those that reveal the ephemeral nature of existence? There are cultures that celebrate certain ideals of perfection (Hellenic Greece and Imperial Rome, for example) and others that relish the melancholy of the passing of things, the transition from perfection (cherry blossom, red maple leaf) to imperfection and finally to a totally withered state, thus valorizing deformity, defect, and blemish: the grain on the wood and the veins on the leaves; the tarnish of the silver and the patina on the bronze; the cracks on the glaze and the shadows on the walls. We often see fruits and flowers menaced by insects in the woodblocks and ink drawings of the great Japanese masters such as Utamaro, just as Western still life painting abounds in leaves damaged by caterpillars, fruit eaten by mice, spiders in waiting. As every fruit lover knows, a melon has not reached its perfect ripeness until the skin begins to show signs of blemish.

It is rare to enter a fine restaurant, upscale shop, Zen temple, or even a traditional home in Japan without seeing both a flower arrangement and a miniature garden. Furthermore, the simple chabana bouquet is essential to the tea ceremony. Even if ignorant of all compositional rules, one would do well to pay close attention to such bouquets, not only for their intrinsic beauty, but also for the manner in which they articulate the space around them. In her study of ikebana, Gusty L. Herrigel reveals the metaphysical dimensions of this art form, which has striking parallels with landscape painting: "In flower arrangements, the empty space left between plants is part of the composition, just as are the plants. They are as important as the three lines of the pattern [sky, man, earth; *shin, sō, gyō*] and by analogy represent the ineffable, the informal, and silence [. . .] Everything is condensed, is concentrated, and takes on a relief within emptiness . . ."[13] Ikebana not only sets a mood but also instantiates an aesthetic, thus it teaches us to see. These bouquets are simultaneously nature stylized to the utmost degree *and* a singular element within the total work of art constituted by a tea room, dining room, or storefront display: simultaneously compositions and symbols, they inspire us to see the natural world anew.

Ikebana is one manner of composing with nature, photography is another. There is an inspiring film by Henri-Georges Clouzot, *Le Mystère Picasso* (1956), in which we see the artist drawing and painting works for the camera. Some of these are done on glass panels, so that the artist can make changes as he progresses, and we view the entire process. Most striking is that even those quite familiar with Picasso's art will probably not be able to ascertain the moment when he deems the picture finished. We believe that he has applied the final stroke to a perfect image, to find that he then makes an erasure and continues. I have had the same experience in the Japanese Galleries of the Metropolitan Museum of Art, where there is usually an ikebana arrangement on display. As I watch the artist place each flower, I try to imagine at what point the bouquet is complete. Never have I guessed correctly. Flower arranging in the West is rarely rule-governed, depending rather on intuition determined by a loose sense of formal possibilities that are rarely if ever prescriptive. To the contrary, ikebana—taught in numerous schools, each with its own style—follows strict principles and protocols determining the choice and combination of flowers, the form of the bouquet, and the appropriate style, size, shape, and placement of the receptacle.

The same considerations obtain for flower arranging as for the tea ceremony: season, weather, time of day; the relation to the image or calligraphy on display, the particularities of the setting, the style of pottery, the aesthetic proclivities of the guests. The chabana may consist of but a single flower, but even so it is caught in a web of symbols and allusions. It is also restricted by the proscription of certain "forbidden flowers," including those with unpleasant names, strong odors, or varieties that are exotic, long-lasting, or without seasonal specificity. The perfection of chabana is illustrated by a famous anecdote concerning Sen no Rikyū, beautifully

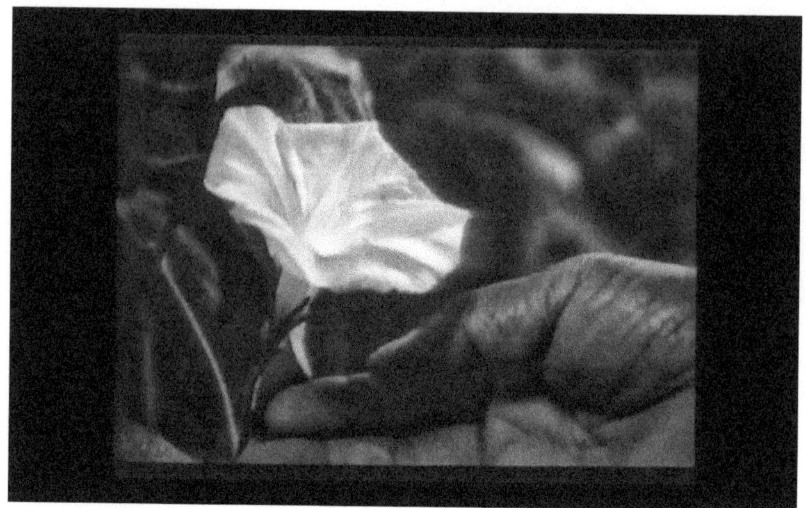

Film still from Teshigahara Hiroshi, Rikyū *(1989).*

depicted in a film by Teshigahara Sōfū's son Hiroshi, best known as a filmmaker for his adaptation of Abe Kōbō's novel *Woman in the Dunes* (book 1962; film 1964). His film *Rikyū* (1989)—produced after he had become master of the Sōgetsu ikebana school following his father Sōfū's death in 1979—begins with Rikyū tending to the magnificent morning glories that surround his tea hut. As he hears that the warlord Hideyoshi is on his way to admire them, he culls a single blossom, and then orders his assistant to remove all the remaining flowers from the bushes. Hideyoshi is infuriated, but as he enters the tea room he understands: on the wall in a woven bamboo basket is that single perfect flower.

Toward the late 1940s, Teshigahara Sōfū—in reaction to traditional wabi-sabi tea aesthetics—radically transformed ikebana, investigating the very limits of the art form: cut flowers displayed directly on the floor or outside in gardens;

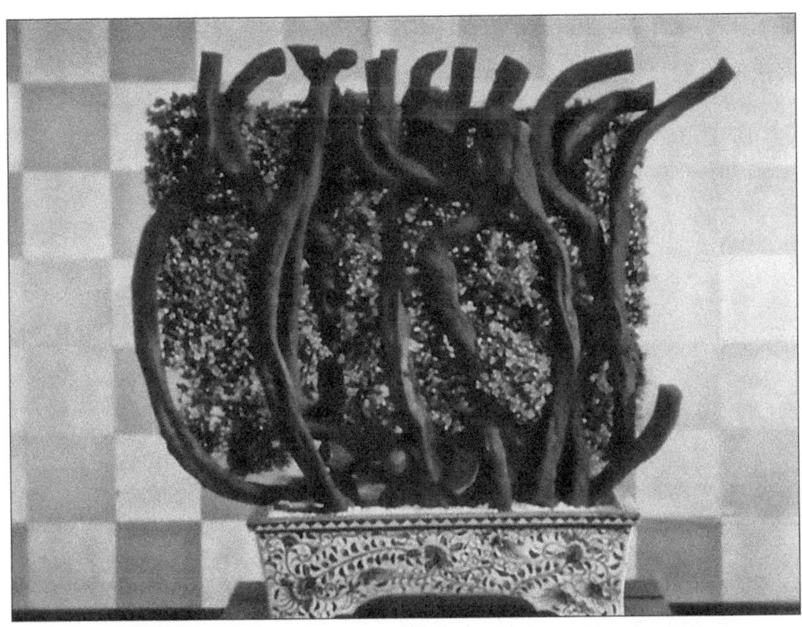

Film still from Teshigahara Hiroshi, Ikebana *(1957): ikebana by Teshigahara Sōfū.*

dried plants, driftwood, and deadwood combined with or used in place of live flowers; vases and bowls replaced by sculptures (including those of artists he befriended, such as Isamu Noguchi and Yagi Kazuo; in turn, Noguchi would occasionally exhibit his ceramics with plant arrangements). Perhaps most radically, he emphasized the very act of arranging flowers as a form of performance. As he also practiced calligraphy, pottery, sculpture, and painting—in all these fields evincing the most contemporary, indeed avant-garde, tendencies—his flower arranging must necessarily be considered in this broader context.[14]

In 1958 Teshigaraha Sōfū inaugurated a new building in Tokyo for his ikebana school and entrusted his son

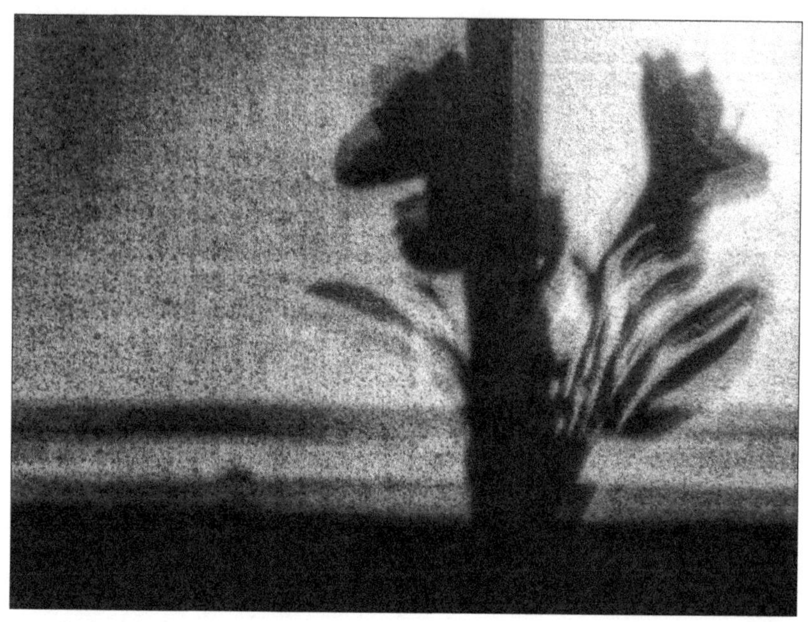

Shadow ikebana.

Hiroshi with organizing an extraordinarily ambitious exhibition and performance program that would come to include nearly all of the great Western artists who visited Japan in the decades to follow, as well as many of the major figures of the various Japanese avant-gardes.[15] The irony is that the main activity of this ikebana school, the art of flower arranging, had no apparent impact on any of the Western artists the school featured. If only that pre-eminent purveyor of Zen-inspired art, John Cage—who performed at Sōgetsu during his first visit to Japan in 1962, when he discovered the garden of Ryōan-ji—had been sufficiently inspired by contemporary manifestations of ikebana so as to have collaborated with Teshigahara father or son! (Cage was renowned as a mycologist, so botany was certainly within his purview.) One can imagine a stage designed by Teshigahara Hiroshi, similar to those he did for open-air operas in Europe in the 1990s, with huge complex bamboo structures, conceived simultaneously as sculpture, setting, and musical instrument, where the waving of the bamboo in the wind would produce "clacks!" that would indeterminately punctuate and syncopate Cage's music and Merce Cunningham's dance.[16] But this was not to be.

Artists have continued to expand the limits of ikebana. One of the most extreme manifestations of this art form exists at the intersection of experimental ikebana, land art, and performance art: Nakagawa Yukio's *Hana Gurui* (Flower Crazy, 2002). Staged on a rainy day upon the bed of the Shinano River in Niigata Prefecture, the work consisted of the ninety-five-year-old co-founder of Butoh, Ohno Kazuo, dancing in a wheelchair, while overhead a helicopter dropped a half-million flower petals upon him. (One might compare, *mutatis mutandis*, Karlheinz Stockhausen's 1995 musical composition *Helikopter-Streichquartett*.) Personally, I favor much more intimate ikebana, to the point where, inspired by an autumnal haiku by Morikawa Kyoriku (1656–1715), student and collaborator of Bashō, I had imagined a series of totally immaterial, aleatory, evanescent "shadow ikebana."

> *On the balustrade,*
> *ever-lengthening shadows*
> *of chrysanthemum*[17]

I thought that I had invented a new form of this art until I discovered Lafcadio Hearn's *Glimpses of Unfamiliar Japan* (1894), where we find the following description of an ikebana exhibition: "You will also observe how much the white or pale blue screen behind the flowers enhances the effect by lamp or lantern light. For the screen has been arranged with the special purpose of showing the exquisiteness of plant shadows; and the sharp silhouettes of sprays and blossoms cast thereon are beautiful beyond the imagining of any Western decorative artist."[18]

A revolution in ceramics

French artist and critic Michel Tapié—who originated the concept of *art informel* and who was a major figure in the artistic interchange between European and Japanese art in the postwar period—spoke of Teshigahara Sōfū in the same breath as Pablo Picasso and Jackson Pollock.[19] While more orthodox ikebana masters, like their tea ceremony counterparts, were apt to prefer traditional ceramics and art, Teshigahara Sōfū opted for collaborations with avant-garde sculptors and potters. Concerning the latter, in 1948 three potters—Yagi Kazuo, Suzuki Osamu, Yamada Hikaru—founded Sōdeisha (literally the "Crawling through the Mud Association"). Under the influence of Western ceramists—notably Picasso, Miró, and later Noguchi—they embraced international modernism, yet they were unwilling to abandon their identity as potters and began to create equivocal objects on the border between ceramic sculpture and traditional pottery. For example, the holes on vases were gradually closed off, so that the object, still vaselike in form, could no longer function as a vase yet didn't quite look like a sculpture.[20] The pivotal year for this group was 1954, when Yagi Kazuo created *Mr. Samsa's Walk*, a sort of wheel from which protrude numerous irregularly shaped

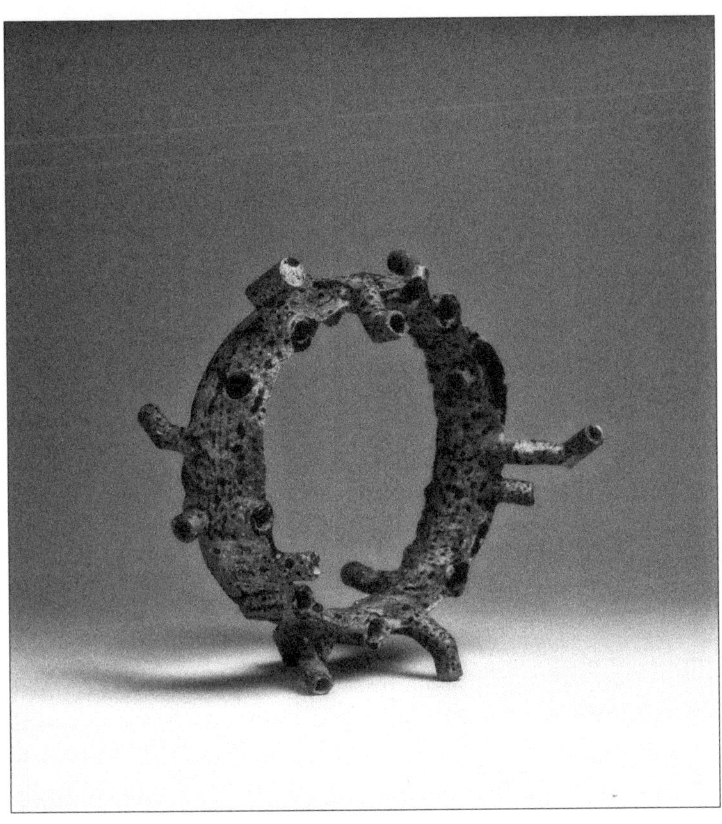

Yagi Kazuo, Mr. Samsa's Walk, *ceramic sculpture (1954).*

tubes—a non-functional abstract work that was particularly shocking in Kyoto, the conservative center of the Japanese pottery world. The piece in time became perhaps the most famous work of modernist Japanese ceramics.[21]

I felt certain that this work among all others would be showcased in the MoMA *Tokyo 1955–1970* exhibition, especially since Yagi was already represented in the MoMA collections. The Museum of Modern Art has generally sequestered the ceramics that enter their collections within their Architecture and Design department, where they are displayed as instantiations of "industrial design," thus not quite as "art." "Studio" pottery, like all "craft," was—with some exceptions, notably Art Nouveau and Art Deco— anathema to the MoMA aesthetic and thus for the most part excluded.[22]

It is, of course, hardly surprising to find that MoMA's history of the Japanese avant-garde should be aligned with, and assimilated to, its view of Modernism in general. MoMA's *The New Japanese Painting and Sculpture* (1966) was one of the first major exhibitions in the West on the theme, and given the title of the show, the perspective on ceramics was unequivocal: if present, it would be categorized as sculpture. The show in fact included four ceramic pieces by Yagi Kazuo, including *A Cloud Remembered* (1962) from the MoMA collection. These works, along with two terra cotta pieces by the lesser-known Tsuji Shindō—a Zen priest whose work influenced Yagi and the Sōdeisha group—would be the only ceramics in that exhibition. However, there is no mention in the catalogue of the realm of ceramics, since the pieces in question were unequivocally considered to be "sculptures" (and thus "art" rather than "craft," if one wishes to maintain the then operative distinction).[23]

Both Sōdeisha and MoMA wished to realign traditional categories, but for different reasons. The Sōdeisha group went to great pains to differentiate their works from modernist sculpture, precisely in order to remain within the world of pottery (*yakimono*, "fired things"), going so far as to create a new term for such creations, *obuje-yaki* (fired object, a portmanteau word derived from *objet*, the French term for object, and *yaki*, the Japanese word for firing). They saw themselves as potters working at the formal limits of ceramics. To the contrary, MoMA saw them—when the works in question were non-functional—as modernist sculptors working in clay. Thus the inclusion of such artists in MoMA exhibitions was done in such a way as to omit the complex history and aesthetic specificity of Japanese ceramics. The same problematic would have been treated quite differently by Japanese artists and art critics of the period, for each culture has its own version of modernism, and these sundry modernisms are rarely homologous or synchronized.

Such blind spots are sometimes unconscious acts and sometimes voluntary strategies, as in MoMA's imposition of the long-standing template of a decidedly international modernism on all newcomers. In contrast, the Guggenheim Museum exhibition, *Japanese Art after 1945: Scream against the Sky* (1994), included Teshigahara Sōfū and Yagi Kazuo, as well as Osamu Noguchi, whose pottery—inspired by both a passion for Jōmon culture and an equally strong distaste for what he saw as the decadence of the wabi-sabi tea ceremony aesthetic—greatly influenced the first generation of postwar Japanese avant-garde potters. The curator, Alexandra Munroe, offers the rationale for the exclusion of modernist Japanese calligraphy, flower arranging, and functional ceramics from Western histories of modernism: "Despite the innovative theory and practice of avant-garde traditional arts groups in the postwar period, they have ultimately remained excluded from the international modern art canon because they were perceived as being 'traditional' and therefore 'antimodern' and 'anti-Western.'"[24]

The oxymoron "avant-garde traditional arts" tells the whole story, which can be summed up by the fact that the respective Western and Japanese aesthetic canons are fundamentally incomparable and incompatible. One resultant injustice is that so many Japanese artists who have attempted to engage with Western art are seen abroad as merely derivative of European and American traditions, while many who have received recognition abroad have done so precisely because of those traditional characteristics that have remained in their works, regardless of the extent to which these artists rebelled against such traditionalism. Japanese modernism is most often perceived in the West according to Western modernist categories and stereotypes that generally expunge the complex culturally specific relations between traditional and modernist Japanese art, ignoring the consequent critique of Western modernism by Japanese artists and critics alike. This is, in fact, a global aesthetic problem, and it should serve as a cautionary tale for every traveler, since it reveals how the formation of aesthetic perceptions and choices radically differs from culture to culture.[25]

Postwar modernity and modernization offered new narratives, new forms, and new materials to both traditional and modernist practices, and previously "ignoble" materials found their way into the museum in both Japan and the West. Concrete is a prime example. The widespread use of cast reinforced concrete in architecture—a staple of modernist architecture, ennobled by Le Corbusier—came late to Japan, a result of the rapid reconstruction during the American Occupation, exemplified by the works of Tange Kenzō and Andō Tadao, many of whose major buildings utilized that material. Once new forms and materials are admitted into the realm of a centuries-old traditional culture, anything is possible. In the West, for example, it didn't take very long for weathered Corten steel—which forms a rust-like coating after a certain period of weathering—to become a major design element. But I wonder, however, whether in the Japanese context it will ever be possible for concrete—certainly not a traditional material—to accrue sabi, as the cracked walls, stained by water and pollution, begin to show signs of age.

The problem is further complicated as a result of the internationalization of the art world, as evidenced in the domain of Japanese pottery, which has partially interiorized the Western dichotomies of traditional/avant-garde and functional/sculptural. Pottery specialist and gallerist Aoyama Wahei explains that in many Japanese museums, as well as in influential ceramics journals such as *Honoho Geijutsu*, potters of modern sculptural and conceptual ceramics are generally favored over traditional ceramists making functional works. "This emphasis on the current vogue towards an 'international' style of pottery seems to trump or usurp the position and importance of some potters who make pots in a 'traditional heritage' style unique to Japan."[26] By limiting what is considered "contemporary" or "modern" to conceptual and sculptural styles, many traditional potters of utilitarian works are overlooked for the sake of artists whose ceramics are non-utilitarian and abstract, fitting for international museum exhibition and consequently supported by the critical and museological ceramics establishment.

Aoyama rightly concludes by insisting that "Contemporary means 'the present day, the current, the modern.' The word does not contain the evaluative labels of 'avant-garde, sculptural, conceptual or non-functional.'"[27] In the broadest sense, we can speak of works that are (a) traditional, (b) traditional with innovative aspects, (c) innovative with

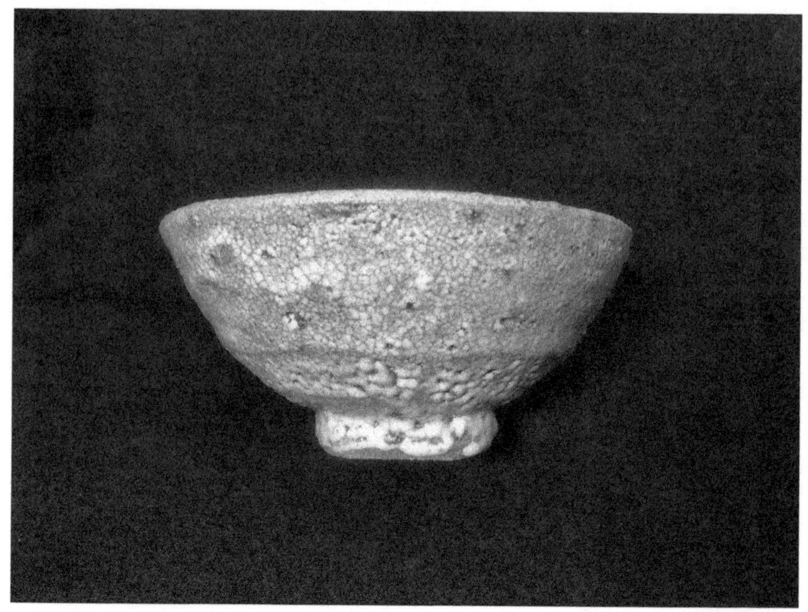

Sakazuki, *Oketani Yasushi; this piece resembles the famed Kizaemon-ido tea bowl, down to its imperfections.*

traditional aspects, and (d) radically innovative, all the while remembering that these terms themselves are relative, hybrid, ambiguous. There exist avant-gardes derived from indigenous traditions, avant-gardes aligned with international modernism, and avant-gardes that attempt to articulate the traditional and the modernist, the indigenous and the international. But of course, such vocabulary always falls short of the mark: the term "avant-garde" can't possibly speak to all the "isms," schools, movements, tendencies, groups, and affiliations that we use to define and categorize—in short, to make sense of—our diverse aesthetic modernities. As is apparent in contrasting Western and Japanese modernisms, all these terms are fundamentally systems of inclusion and exclusion, often prescriptive or proscriptive rather than descriptive.

Indeed, the ceramics associated with chanoyu are hardly of homogenous style and span the entire gamut from the traditional (itself once a source of innovative) and the avant-garde (already being quickly incorporated into the tradition). Even the ardent opponents of the wabi-sabi aesthetic—from the early-20th-century proponents of folk art in the Mingei movement to the mid-20th-century Sōdeisha artists inspired by international modernism—have been embraced by the world of chanoyu. Philosopher and founder of the Mingei folk art movement Yanagi Sōetsu (1889–1961) claimed that "If we want to see a thing well, we must use it well."[28] One might add that we must also learn the different ways of seeing that permit us to look at it well.

There are many modes of art appreciation. We in the West are used to visiting museums to see our favorite masterpieces time and again; tea aficionados might see a given masterpiece but once in a lifetime, or perhaps only in illustrations. Many of the greatest works of Japanese art are veiled in secrecy, hidden in temple storerooms, to be displayed once a year in the annual airing ceremony, if at all.[29] This approach is perfectly congruent with the precepts of the tea ceremony, each of which is ideally a once-in-a-lifetime gathering—*ichigo ichie* (one time, one meeting)—conducted at a specific time for a select group of people, with the objects chosen accordingly. Tea practitioners keep careful diaries noting all aspects of each and every meeting, especially detailing the utensils used and the art displayed. This offers a precise overview of the event, since the particular relations between objects set the tone of each ceremony.

The Japanese have a word for this talent, *toriawase*, the

art of relating objects, poetic allusions, and seasonal symbols, a combinatory skill that by extension also informs the table settings of the kaiseki meal.[30] It is ironic, however, that an aesthetic in which an object is valorized according to its surroundings is also one in which the value of that very same object is augmented by secrecy, by its very withdrawal from the world. In Japan—despite the spate of art museums created in recent years—many of the greatest masterpieces remain in temples, palaces, and private collections inaccessible to the public, and are thus rarely visible. Most travelers to Japan will not even know what they are missing.[31]

In the West, modern aesthetic judgment has been part of the public sphere, effectuated by art historians, critics, gallerists, and collectors, generally concerning works to a great extent visible in public museums, galleries, and other public spaces such as churches, business office lobbies, and hotels. The public exhibition of a work, and its illustrated presence in a catalogue or critical volume, generally increases its value. In Japan, the aesthetic of tea culture has long been exceedingly private, established by exclusive ceremonies limited to a very few people, communicated in private diaries that are rarely shared, and to a great extent controlled by the three major tea schools (Omotesenke, Urasenke, Mushanokōjisenke—all directed by descendants of Sen no Rikyū).

The value of a work is a matter of provenance, a form of authenticity determined not by academic scholarship or scientific investigation but by the connoisseurship of the great tea masters. Yanagi Sōetsu stated this most succinctly: "With these men, seeing was identical with creating [. . .] Seeing led them to using, and using led to seeing still deeper."[32] The connoisseurship necessary to practice chanoyu is the central determinant of aesthetics, essentially a form of criticism-in-action. Yanagi continues, stating the four essential precepts of the way of tea: "Harmony, reverence, purity, and serenity are the inculcated traditional principles of Tea. But these demand spiritual preparation."[33] Such spiritual discipline—which derives from the exigencies of Zen Buddhism and which demands aesthetic connoisseurship—is incumbent upon both host and guest. One must be an active participant in a tea ceremony, and not a mere spectator; one must merit beauty. Hence the nearly insurmountable difficulty for the foreigner who—even if admitted to such events—will most likely not have the aesthetic background, spiritual training, or even the language to actively participate.

Restated in its most general formulation: "The Way of Tea is the law of Beauty."[34] The great tea masters are those with a creative, revolutionary gaze, and their use of a given object guarantees its aesthetic value. This explains the central importance of provenance in Japanese art history. Centuries before Marcel Duchamp's radical claim that it is the artist's choice that creates the work of art, the same sensibility obtained at the 16th-century origins of the modern Japanese tea ceremony. Yanagi: "The founders of the Way of Tea did not see things by means of convention; rather, it was their vision that brought the rules and conventions into being."[35] This fundamental creativity may occur at the moment an object is chosen as worthy of chanoyu (such as the repurposing of Korean tea bowls, transforming commonplace objects into masterpieces) or when that object is deployed (according to the art of toriawase, which establishes the relations between objects in the broader symbolism of the ceremony). This suggests a sort of hermeneutic circle concerning matters of quality and aesthetic value: a particular work is chosen by a tea master due to its greatness, and it is deemed great because it was chosen by a tea master.

Connoisseurship is both intuitive and conventional, and even when one is familiar with the codified aesthetic conventions it is often difficult to say why regarding ceramics one particular curve of a lip, swirl in a pool, or carved foot is more beautiful than another; why a particular sesame (*goma*) ash glaze pattern on a work of Bizen pottery or a particular "dragonfly eye" (*biidoro*)—the vitrified flowing glaze on an Iga piece—is of just the right form; or why the fire color (*hi-iro*) and scorch marks (*koge*) on a Shigaraki work might be exemplary. One can find a dragonfly eye to be beautifully shaped, well placed, of limpid translucidity and attractive color, but the ultimate judgment is a matter of convention as much as intuition, and the borderline between creativity and mannerism is often very vague. Furthermore, mannerism itself is not necessarily a bad thing. In any case, such judgments are tantamount to the sharing of a vision—sometimes across centuries—that entails both work and play, conservation and creativity.

Today, the extent to which context and conditions of display have a role in such choices is crucial. Certain contemporary Japanese works are stunning when exhibited in Western galleries and museums, while others tend to disappear into the background. One example is the phenomenal rise of Kuwata Takurō, whose ceramic works—regularly featured in art journals and international art fairs—are considered by some to be at the summit of contemporary ceramics. The bright primary and artificial colors, gold and platinum details, outlandishly thick glazes, and outrageously

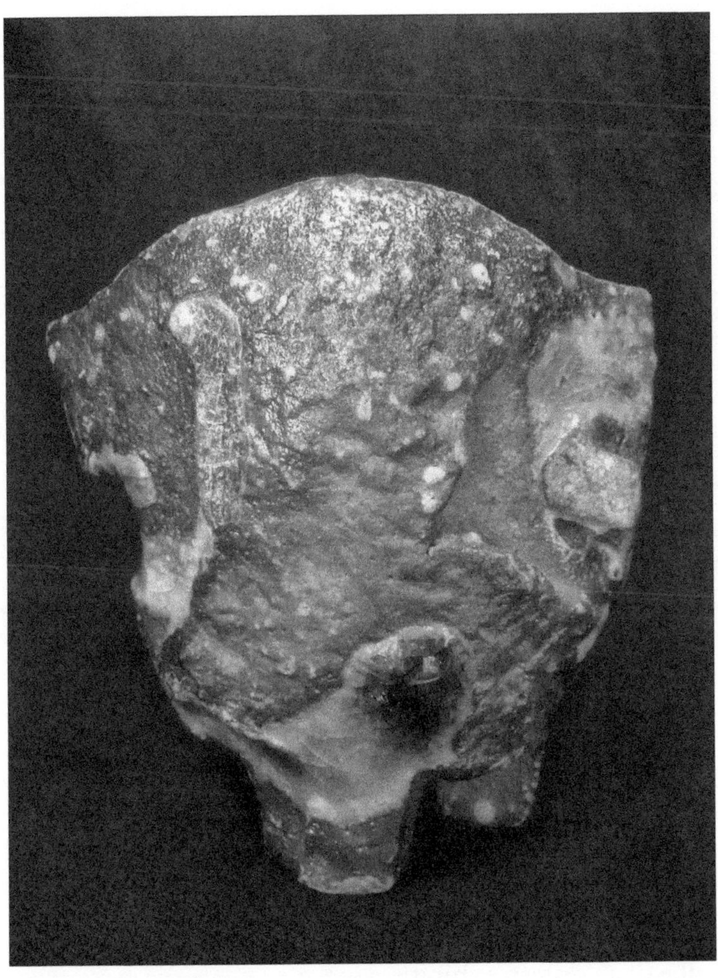

Guinomi, *Fujioka Shūhei.*

distorted shapes are exceptionally eye-catching, visible clear across a brightly lit gallery space. One might contrast Kuwata's piece, with its exaggerated thick white glaze and artificial bright red color, to the other work illustrated here,

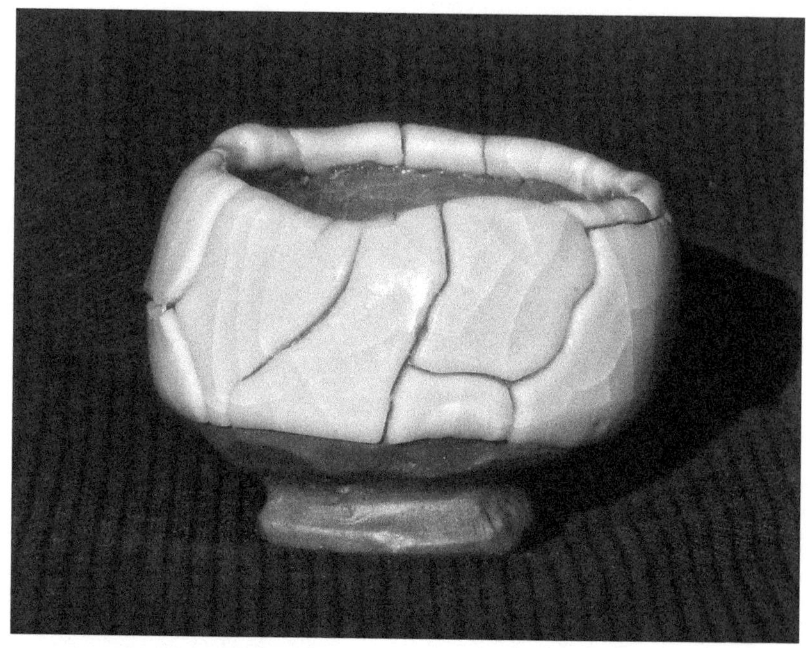

Guinomi, *Kuwata Takurō*.

by the equally innovative Kakurezaki Ryūichi, whose sculptural forms have revolutionized Bizen ceramics. Perfectly attuned to the natural wood colors and subdued lighting of a Japanese gallery, tea room, or restaurant, they would almost disappear in the glare of the panoptically lit white cube of a Western exhibition space.

"Modernity" is originally a Western notion, and Western museums have long been the arbiters of precisely what types of objects get tagged with this nomenclature. Upon inspection one finds chronological and categorial discrepancies between the "modernisms" of many non-Western nations and that of the West, differences that must be remembered when considering Japanese art in the period

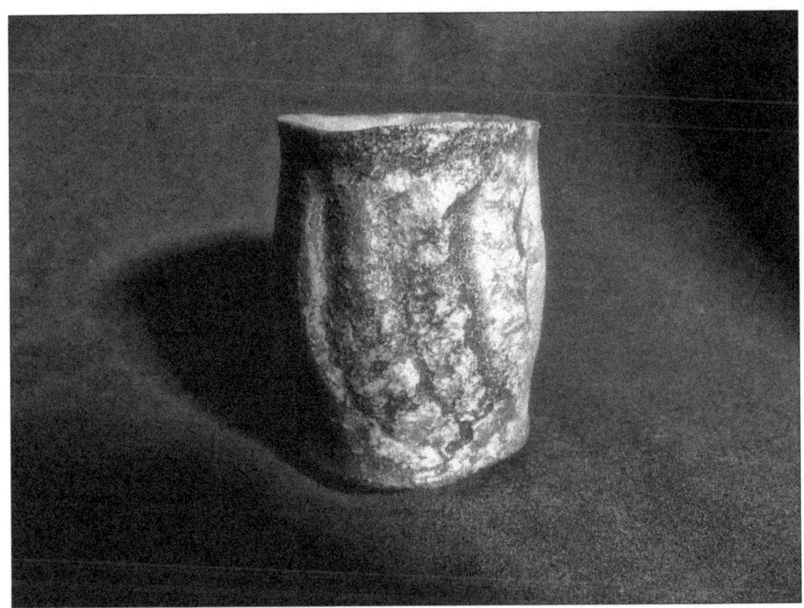

Guinomi, *Kakurezaki Ryūichi.*

under consideration. For centuries Japan had assimilated and transformed Chinese and Korean art in an atmosphere more of appropriation than exchange. This was followed by the two and a half centuries of the Edo period when the country was almost completely closed to foreign exchange, and during which the arts and crafts operated within a conservative master (*iemoto*) and apprentice system, within which constant perfecting of exemplary works and styles, rather than radical innovation, was the norm.

A status quo of normative values had thus endured for centuries in this traditionalist and long authoritarian society, where the values of collective harmony were esteemed far above those of individual expression. Consequently, the *transmission* of perfected techniques, forms, and values was of greater import than their radical *transformation*.[36] This all changed at the beginning of the Meiji period in 1868 with the opening of Japan to Western nations, an intense period of modernization, industrialization, and westernization. From that moment on, Japan went through alternating cycles of assimilation and rejection of Western values, resulting in constantly shifting debates concerning modernism in the arts: endless experimentation with Western artistic forms and aesthetic concepts countered by periodic quests for uniquely Japanese origins and forms of expression. It is not surprising that many of the most important modernist works of Japanese art are those that interiorized this dichotomy.[37]

A collector's fantasy

Different protocols of experiencing art in different cultures may give rise to great misunderstandings. In Japan, to confine a traditional tea bowl, vase, or sake cup to a museum vitrine would be a misjudgment of values: alienated from use, made blatantly visible by direct lighting while having been created to exist in shadow, deprived of mystery by being constantly on view. A work of art demands a proper mode of encounter, vision, touch (if permitted), contemplation, rememoration. Indeed, to repeat Yanagi Sōetsu's claim concerning functional aesthetic objects such as tea bowls, "if we want to see a thing well, we must use it well."[38] While pottery in Western museums never leaves the showcases, in Japanese museums, thanks to the often-present tea room, even the rarest works occasionally come to life in a tea ceremony, if only for the privileged few. Curators in the West are only beginning to address such issues—particularly exacerbated regarding sacred objects that have been repurposed as "art"—so we are perhaps at the cusp of new ways of approaching such artifacts.[39]

I have an obsessive collector's fantasy. I intend to acquire 365 ceramic sake cups by contemporary artists to eventually create a calendar matching each cup to a specific day of the year, following the same precepts central to the tea ceremony. My project would require, with each daily choice, a certain degree of representational—or at least metaphorical—endeavor, as analogies would be sought between the characteristics of the ceramics and the changing seasonal and atmospheric conditions. This is not so strange in the Japanese context, as there exists the practice of creating a different ikebana every day of the year, or choosing a specific *wagashi* (Japanese tea sweet) daily and matching it to an appropriate dish. This is inspired by the fundamental precept of the tea ceremony, ichigo ichie (one time, one meeting), which insists that each ceremony should be conceived and treasured as unrepeatable, as a once-in-a-lifetime experience, an aestheticized form of *carpe diem*. I am aware of the absurdity of this task, not unlike that of the Tokyo restaurateur who tries to match a specific cup to a specific sake, a *reductio ad absurdum* of the most blatant sort, however amusing may be the process. Indeed, given the perpetually changing weather, light, mood, and so forth, one would need to continually redo such a list! I was amused to discover that art historian Aby Warburg reorganized his vast library at the beginning of each new research project, believing that for a library to be alive the order of the books must be constantly changed, akin to the manner in which art collectors and museum curators rotate the works in their collections.

Hans Ulrich Obrist suggests that "Collection-making,

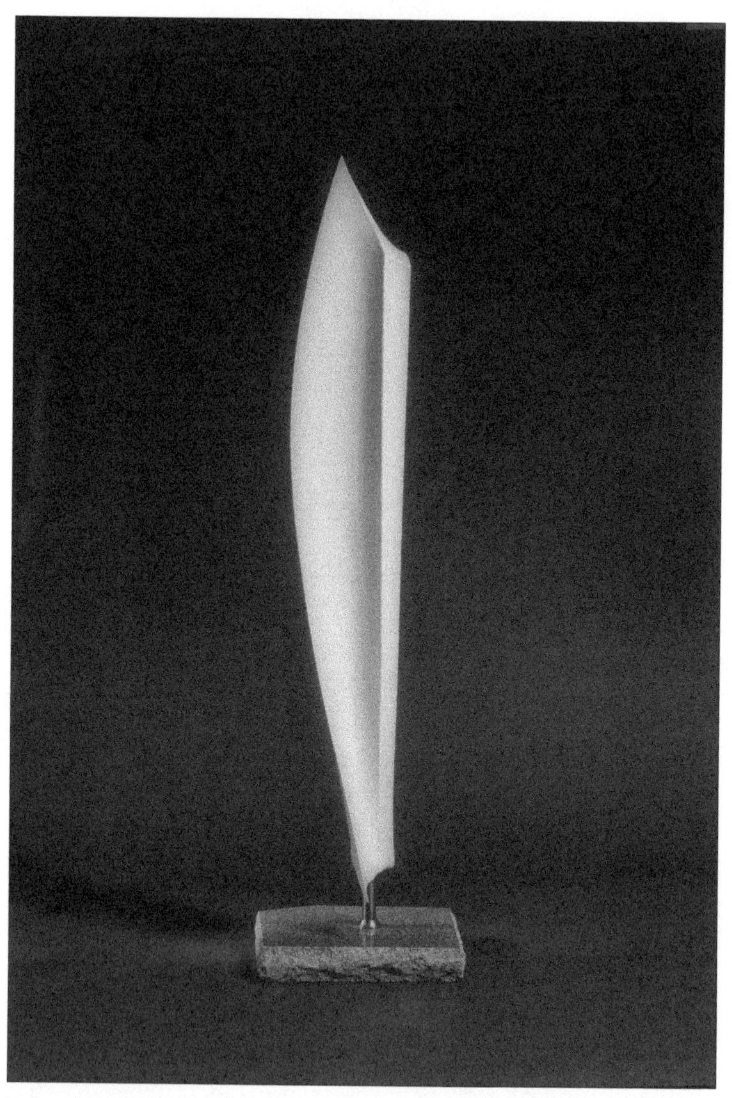

Fukami Sueharu, Upright (Kitsu), ceramic sculpture, 197.5 cm (2012).

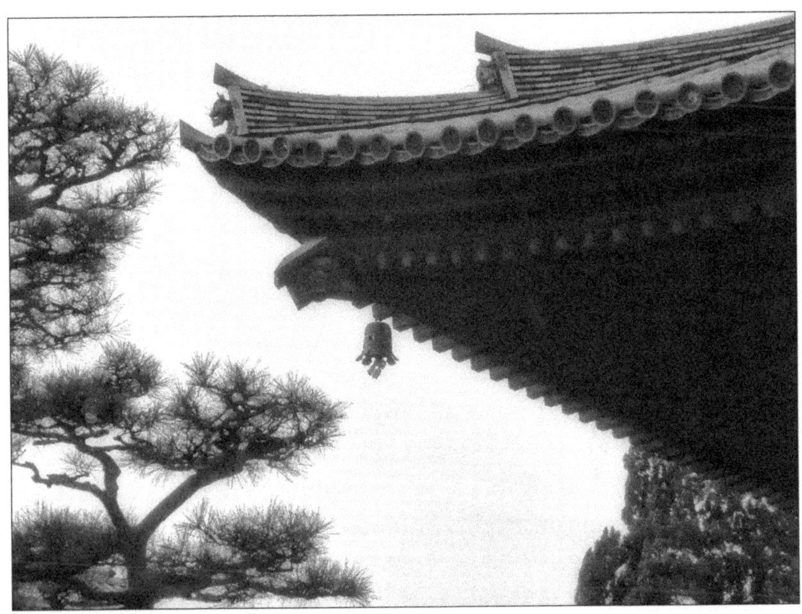

Tōfuku-ji.

you could say, is a method of producing knowledge."[40] To test this hypothesis, I would like to ask the reader to perform a simple mental experiment in order to consider the extent to which context influences the experience of an art work, and even more emphatically, to learn how to *unlearn* patterns of vision that might blind us to alternate ways of seeing, so as to prepare us for culture shock. Consider the extremely large (198 cm. tall) ceramic sculpture long exhibited in the Japanese Galleries of the Metropolitan Museum of Art, *Upright* (2012), by renowned contemporary ceramist Fukami Sueharu.[41] Its continued presence in these galleries is in itself an important curatorial statement. This work may be likened to something created in a wind tunnel to visualize the forms of air flow, or it may be compared to the curves of traditional Japanese swords (many of which are National Treasures that have a large role in the Japanese imagination) or to the curves of the rooftops of the structures at Tōfuku-ji temple in Kyoto. Or, if we consider that the piece was part of the exhibit *Birds in the Art of Japan* (Metropolitan Museum of Art, 2013), it would be impossible not to discern a family resemblance with Constantin Brancusi's *Bird in Space* (1923). We reach the limits of representation, a necessity in examining cultural differences of aesthetic vision.

The first, and most obvious, part of our experiment would be to mentally shift Fukami's work from the Japanese Galleries to those of Modern and Contemporary Art, where it would indeed sit perfectly alongside the Met's marble version of *Bird in Space*. However, in these galleries almost totally bereft of ceramics as well as of Japanese art, the presence of *Upright* would be a reminder of the chasm separating these two cultures, both in terms of the aesthetic status of ceramics and the place of Japanese art in the Western modernist canon. To continue the experiment, try and imagine its incongruous appearance as a guest visitor in the Gallery of American Ceramics, a reminder that the forms and techniques of Japanese art often infiltrate Western creativity, and vice versa. To continue the experiment, now place *Upright* in more appropriate surroundings, within one of the few vitrines featuring contemporary ceramics on The Great Hall Balcony, where it would find a logical though limiting context. It finally returns to the Japanese Galleries, where it now appears somewhat ill at ease among the wabi-sabi objects, *ukiyo-e* woodblocks, theatrical kimono, and decorative screens. For the moment, only the Noguchi fountain, a few pieces of contemporary ceramics, and an occasional sword resonate.

Radical ceramics

There are category errors that deceive and disappoint (like mine concerning the photographs of Jōmon pottery) and category errors that enlighten. The Gutai movement, founded in Osaka in 1954—the year that Yagi created *Mr. Samsa's Walk*—is characterized by its extreme, scandalous, and often violent rejection of traditional Japanese culture. In the West it is usually referred to as the first Japanese avant-garde movement—certainly because of its performative excesses—even though it originated years after Sōdeisha, Sōgetsu, and other radically innovative groups. One might more properly say that it was the first Japanese avant-garde to eschew the formalities of traditional Japanese art and align itself with what was becoming a Western-oriented and increasingly New York–centric internationalism. Thus one would not expect to find any ceramics in the *Gutai: Splendid Playground* exhibition at the Guggenheim Museum (2013), yet the show suggests, though quite indirectly, a provocative manner of reconsidering ceramics through a consideration of the limits of performance.

Featured in that exhibition is the most famous of the Gutai artists, Shiraga Kazuo, now celebrated for the many exuberant, dynamic abstract works painted with his feet, a scandal at the time. In 1955, the moment he became associated with the Gutai group he created his most famous work, *Challenging Mud*, which was to establish the paradigm for his later paintings. Performed during the First Gutai Art Exhibition that took place at the Ohara Kaikan ikebana school in Tokyo (along with the more famous Sōgetsu school, known for its support of the avant-garde), the artist rolled around half naked in a pile of mud, which remained on view during the entire exhibition. The work itself was not afterward preserved, and only photographic documentation remains, thus one must wonder whether what we now see is the documentation of a performance, the trace of a lost work of art, the photograph itself as art work, or an equivocal amalgam of these possibilities.

This image appears in every major survey of postwar Japanese art, and it is always described in terms familiar to Western histories of modernism. The Guggenheim *Gutai* catalogue speaks of Shiraga as "staging actions that used the body as a medium" and characterizes the imagery as "performance views," all the while maintaining the ambiguity between performance and art work, with the term "work" used simultaneously and ambiguously as verb and noun. Thus the "relics" of the performance were left as "artworks in their own right for the duration of the show, expanding the borders of what could constitute painting."[42] These equivocations are reinforced by the fact that the *Gutai* catalogue has an entire chapter on "Performance Painting: Pictures with Time and Space." We are consequently motivated to consider these actions/performances/works in relation to Jackson Pollock's "action painting" (1950s) and Yves Klein's later *Anthropométries* series (1960s), events where nude women made imprints with paint on canvas, which subsequently constituted material art works. In relation to Shiraga's later oil paintings done by foot, we may even speak in terms beyond "action" and "performance," as dance theorist André Lepecki suggests: "Painting will not escape the call of the choreographic."[43] Or as ceramist Koie Ryōji exclaimed: "To understand clay, you must have eyes not only in your fingernails but in your toenails too."[44]

Inspired by such malleability and permeability of categories, we might consider a totally different paradigm in which to place Shiraga's *Challenging Mud*, a radically new genealogy, that of ceramics, construed in the broadest sense of the term. For in the Japanese context, ceramics—that art made of mud—will also not escape the call of "choreography," since that term can well be used to describe the ritualistic gestures of the tea ceremony as well as more generally the gestural etiquette of the arts of the table, both of which are dependent upon pottery. Furthermore, by the 1950s, some potters, most famously Peter Voulkos in the USA, offered potting demonstrations as veritable performances.

In the overview of modern artists working in clay included in the provocative book edited by Simon Groom, *A Secret History of Pottery*, British potter and author Edmund de Waal cites the work of phenomenological philosopher Maurice Merleau-Ponty in suggesting that "every perception is a communion and a coition of our body with things," permitting de Waal to rethink that epistemological claim in terms of the aesthetics of ceramics: "This coition of the body is one of the secret stories of the century of artists working with clay; it reveals what can be described as a phenomenological approach to clay. For some artists using clay has been the recuperation of unmediated materiality: they had a powerful sense of clay as earth, as being the great formless primal matter that allowed them a kind of expression they could not approach through other materials."[45] This phenomenological approach suggests the fundamental importance of the performative in relation to ceramics. He then alludes to the viscerality of a "returning to earth" in terms of overcoming the alienation from land and culture typical of the 20th century.

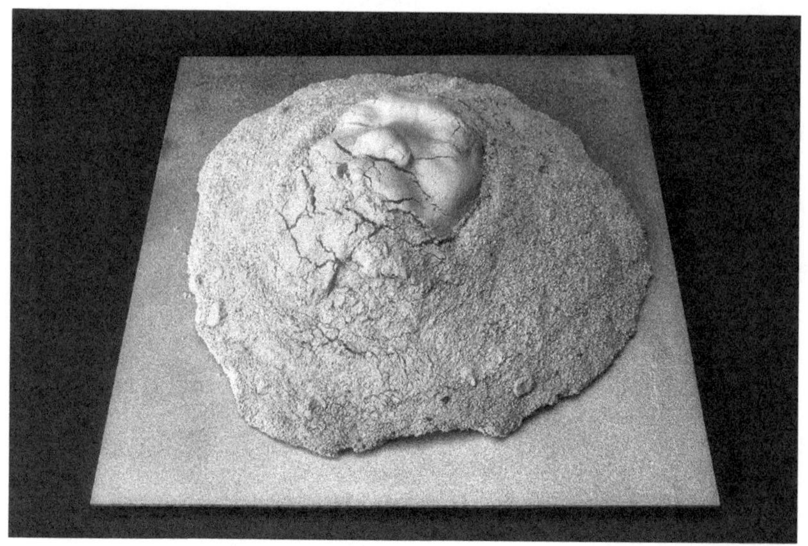

Koie Ryōji, Return to the Earth *(detail, 1971).*

It is curious that at this point de Waal does not mention Koie Ryōji's most famous work, *Return to the Earth* (1971)—perhaps the first instance of ceramics as performance art—which he surely knows. This work consists of a series of small mounds made of the powder derived from totally pulverized white ceramic toilet bowls, each mound forming an impression of the artist's face molded by a mask, with the images becoming successively less and less distinct, such that the final one is indistinguishable from a simple mound of powder. While the work is superficially related to the serialism and minimalism central to the Western avant-garde of the period, and while it certainly alludes (perhaps ironically) to Duchampian aesthetics by the use of the pulverized toilets, this radical gesture more pointedly highlights the tensions and contradictions within the contemporary world of Japanese pottery, the oppositions of which may be outlined as follows: mass produced / handmade; damage / perfection; found object / created work; materiality / expression; tradition / innovation; ceramics / sculpture; object / performance.

The elision of Koie's *Return to the Earth* from de Waal's analysis is perhaps simple oversight, but it appears strategic, for its presence would suggest a very different, indeed antithetical, realignment of aesthetic categories. And so de Waal avoids these complications, which would in turn overly complicate his phenomenologically based argument, and at this point he presents a photograph of Shiraga's performance, now translated as *Wrestling in the Mud*, thus by linguistic association recalling Sōdeisha, which literally means "crawling through the mud." Shiraga revealed that mud may be a material for painting, and painting a form of performance. Koie complicated the relations between ceramics and sculpture, and showed how both can be forms of performance. Following these artists as well as de Waal, we may imagine an aesthetic where mud is a prelude to ceramics, and performance a possible fate for pottery. Between Shiraga and Koie, between the raw and the cooked, between the moist mass of clay before it is formed and the hard clay collapsed to amorphousness after being subjected to the extreme limits of fire, between two types of formlessness, is to be found—literally inspired by a *nostalgie de la boue*—the expanded performative essence of pottery.

3

Perfect Offerings

THE RESTAURANT

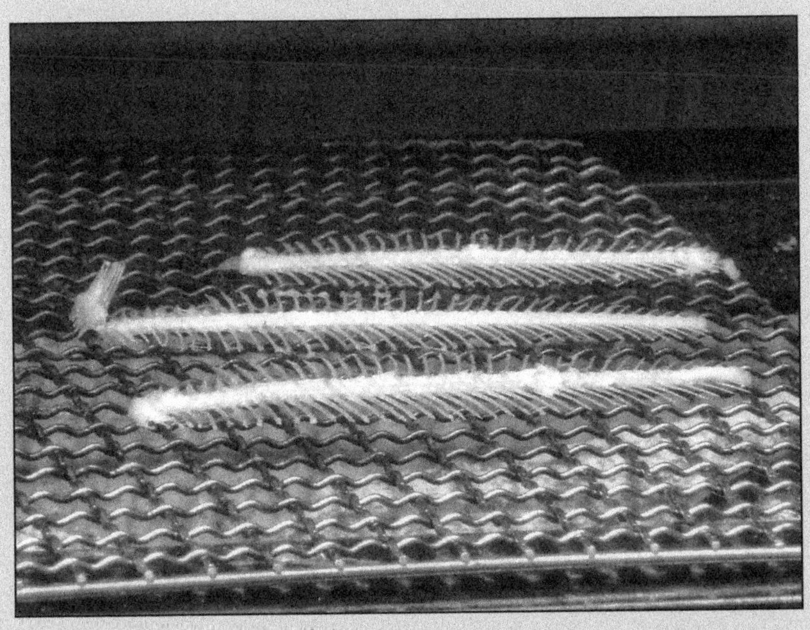

Grilled fish bones, Sōjiki Nakahigashi restaurant, Kyoto.

Even in Kyoto,
hearing the cuckoo's cry,
I long for Kyoto.
  Matsuo Bashō

Gifts may be gauged by degrees of generosity, perfection, and inventiveness. In the Kyoto apartment where I would spend a memorable New Year's Day in communion with Tanizaki Jun'ichirō is a scroll whose calligraphy reads 海如酒, "Sake like the ocean." This hyperbolic simile, which probably once graced the walls of a sake bar (*izakaya*), offers most cheerful welcome. Rice was for centuries the culinary staple, the economic foundation, and the symbolic nexus of Japanese culture. Some even believe that every grain of rice is a Bodhisattva. During the New Year season, many Shinto shrines display huge bales of rice and multitudes of bottles of sake they have received as gifts. In smaller shrines the offerings are more modest, though no less symbolic. At Otoyo-jinja located along the Philosopher's Path, for example, two sculptures of rats flank the main altar—where a modest offering of fruits and vegetables is displayed—one rat holding a sake bowl, the other a scroll, symbols of material well-being and cultural achievement.

I have always wondered about the quality of the sake in the endless cups offered to shrines, to ancestors' tombs, and to sculptures of the Bodhisattva Jizō throughout Japan, but in any case it is clear that in a more mundane context, the Japanese occasionally seek heights of rather absurd perfection, as in 2016 when a bunch of grapes of the Ruby Roman variety sold for 1.1 million yen (about $10,000) and in 2015 when two melons went for 1.5 million yen (about $13,000).

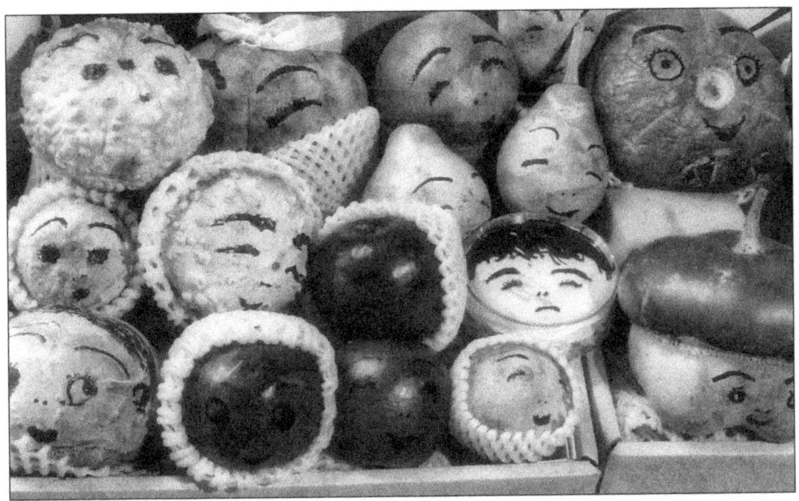

Painted gourds, Nishiki Market, Kyoto.

There are, however, more poetic manifestations of culinary perfection. In the section of Sei Shōnagon's *Pillow Book* where she enumerates "Adorable Things," she begins by noting "The face of a child drawn on a melon."[1] I was not all that surprised when one day I came across, in Kyoto's Nishiki Market, a vegetable stand with a box full of gourds, each one painted with the caricature of a child's face.

One November evening at the eponymous Kyoto restaurant Hayashi, where our party took up five of the seven seats at the counter, I requested permission to photograph the dishes. Chef Hayashi quite imperatively insisted that I not take out my camera, so as to concentrate on the meal. He was, in a certain sense, correct. During that meal with my friends, the pottery specialists and tea practitioners Umeda Mitsuko and Umeda Minoru, we were served a whole grilled *tai* (sea bream), among the great delicacies of Japan, and at one point Mitsuko removed a small bone with her

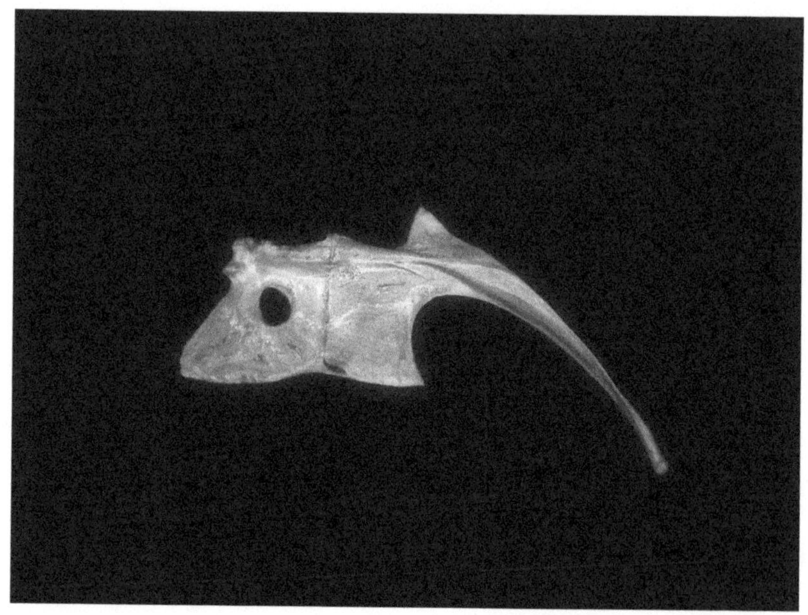

Bone from tai *fish (pagrus major, red sea bream) painted gold.*

chopsticks and showed me how its shape resembled that of the entire fish, explaining that it is a lucky charm. Mitsuko's English is as impoverished as my Japanese, but we manage to communicate quite well through objects, and as art objects are usually semiotically richer than everyday things, we seem quite able to express our respective aesthetic affinites, at least up to a point. About a week later when I visited their gallery she had a gift for me: beautifully wrapped in a small elegant wooden box was the fish bone, lacquered in gold. What we receive from any significant event depends upon preparation, concentration, and remembrance, the latter existing in the form of memories, photos, and objects. Yet these souvenirs do not only constitute what we take from a site, but also what we give back. For a memory may be an homage, a photo, a work of art, an object, a nexus of relations. We must know not only how to give, but also how to receive, a gift.

• • •

An object may be metaphor, symbol, or allegory; clue, plot, or denouement; trace, paradox, or mystery; magical, mystical, or eschatological. Hence the interest in functional objects, which entail a *de facto* critique of the Kantian notion of an aesthetics based on purposeful purposelessness. In Japan, we are ushered into the most intimate proximity with these objects, exemplified by the appreciation of ceramics, which is grounded in a system of values that operates both in the daily sphere (cuisine) as well as at the highest levels of culture (chanoyu). Few Westerners are prepared for the aesthetic subtleties of such encounters, but that hardly means that appreciation is impossible. To take a familiar situation, consider that a meal in a French haute cuisine restaurant is rarely about the pottery, to the extent that I challenge the reader to cite a single instance when a restaurant's ceramics were memorable, much less the potter recognizable. It is not that ceramics are incidental—many restaurateurs have tableware designed especially for them—but rather that these ceramics are rarely valorized, as they are mainly meant to blend in with the decor and highlight the cuisine. Furthermore, such pieces are more often than not manifestations of industrial design rather than handcraft, for reasons of cost, standardization, and replaceability.[2] Yet this was not always the case.

At the summit of 17th-century court culture under Louis XIV at Versailles, the appreciation of cuisine in France reached a level of magnificence perhaps only matched in the Chinese courts of lore. At that moment, cuisine existed

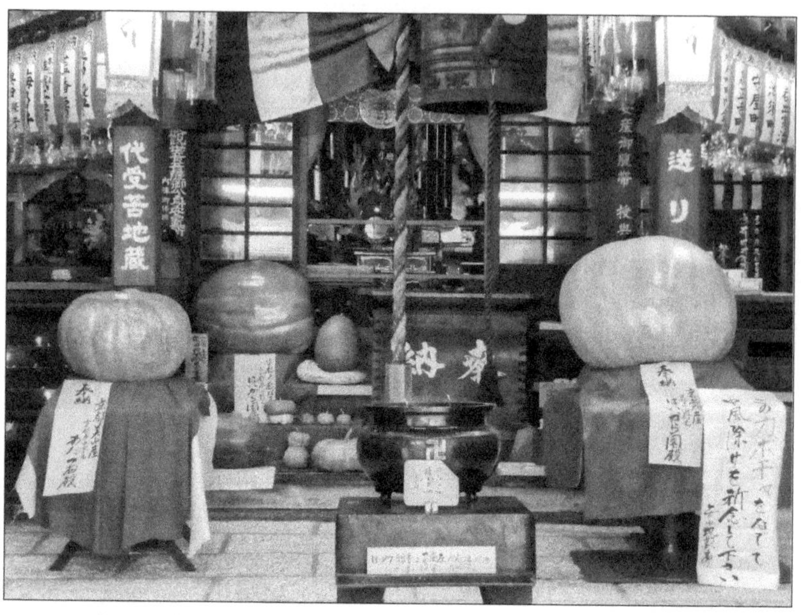
Pumpkins at the Yata-dera temple, Teramachi, Kyoto.

among the arts in common splendor, each art and craft directed by a specific protocol in the service of a highly regulated and codified ritual, all with one goal, the celebration of the divine glory of Le Roi Soleil, the Sun King. During the epoch of the great festivals, the gardens of Versailles were constantly transformed during the staging of these great spectacles—*Les Plaisirs de l'Isle enchantée* (1664), *Le Grand Divertissement royal de Versailles* (1668), and *Les Divertissements de Versailles* (1674)—where cuisine, ceramics, couture, poetry, theater, music, dance, ballet, waterworks, fireworks, and landscaping were all coordinated—chronologically and spatially, dramatically and symbolically—into a total work of art. This holistic model, a prototype of the Gesamtkunstwerk, is most useful in grasping the intermingling of the arts that occurs in the Japanese tea ceremony, the former an epitome of extravagant courtly splendor, the latter a summit of discreet aesthetic luxury.

A distinction in vocabulary will help to sort things out and make comparisons. In the courtly tradition, French meals were served as banquets, with several consecutive services of numerous dishes (*service à la française*). It was only with the widespread appearance of restaurants after the French Revolution that the modern form of sequentially serving a series of single dishes with limited side dishes took hold (*service à la russe*). This is homologous to the 16th-century shift in Japan from Chinese-style courtly banquets to the sequentially organized kaiseki meals inspired by the tea ceremony. (The banquet perdured in miniaturized form as the *bento*, a compartmentalized wood or lacquer box containing tiny portions of all the courses that might typically be served in a kaiseki meal.)[3] These respective shifts entailed not just a reduction in complexity but also a shift from ostentation and ornateness to understatement. It would not be too much of an exaggeration to caricature this by saying that the ideal Japanese decor became sedate wabi-sabi ceramic dishes on a *hinoki* wood table in a minimalist wooden room, while the ideal Western decor eventually evolved to a white plate on a white tablecloth in a white room, akin to the white cube of the modernist gallery. In French haute cuisine, the food—characterized by technical complexity and the condensation of flavors—is the focus; in Japanese kaiseki cuisine, the food—distinguished by the juxtaposition of ingredients in relatively simple preparations intended to accentuate their natural flavors—is carefully matched to the ceramics and the decor, thus becoming part of an aesthetic totality.

The modern Western table setting became a sort of focusing mechanism to foreground the cuisine that gastronomes would insist was well on its way to becoming an autonomous art object. This change was contemporaneous with patterned tableware yielding to—one might even say sublimated into—the standard white or subtly bordered dishes that have long been the paradigm. Consider in this regard the dinner plate in relation to the canvas, all the while remembering the limits of homologies, analogies, and correspondences, as well as the traps of anachronism, for the histories of different art forms are rarely synchronous. The brilliant white field of the plate's lip borders a shallow well, such that the relation of lip and well to food is analogous to that of frame, matting, and canvas to the picture. The plate serves as support, matting, and frame combined. In fact, we might see the thin gold band bordering the lip of a porcelain plate as an allusion to and sublimation of the elaborate gold picture frames typical of 19th-century European art. The dish (in the double sense of plate and food) may be construed as a picture in the still life genre—more or less abstract according to the cuisine—where the food is composed while the plate all but disappears.[4]

Originally, with the advent of easel painting, the frame served an iconographic role as a figurative window onto the depicted world, a mechanism to heighten the realist illusion. However, with the rise of abstraction, the use value of the frame shifted to an ontological function, as it became a sign of the autonomy of the painting itself, setting the painting off from other objects in the room. Finally, near the end of modernism with the rise of Abstract Expressionism, the frame was outmoded and discarded. Given the novelty, equivocation, and sheer bizarreness of certain art works, specific markers were often required to indicate the very presence of art, which might otherwise go unnoticed. This larger "frame" would be standardized as the white cube of the gallery and museum, where the art work would be radically set apart from the world. The picture frame, like the dinner plate, is far from neutral: some are meant to be seen, like those baroque gilt frames so out of favor these days, analogous to fabulously decorated Meissen porcelain dishes; others are meant to disappear into the decor, like the thin black metal frames—an appendage of international modernist design—ubiquitous in museums today and analogous to undecorated dishes in Western restaurants.

The aesthetic and ontological aspects of the frame have long been a subject of art historical speculation. In *Pathologie du cadre* (2020), a recent study of the topic in relation to Art Brut—where framing is often subverted—Michel Thévoz parses out the semiological status of the frame by asking: ". . . is it constitutively included or excluded from the field of representation? If neither one nor the other, must it be considered as an intermediary fringe? If it is neither diegetic nor adiegetic, would it be paradiegetic? Or *metadiegetic* (an interrogation of the image concerning its proper functioning, through the experience of its limits)?"[5] In other words, is the frame part of the narration implied by the image, or simply the limit of the tale, or rather something alongside but unrelated to it, or finally perhaps a reflexive comment on the tale itself? He continues: "And what is to be understood by 'frame': the immaterial rectangular contour of a sheet of paper or canvas, or the protective and/or decorative artifact with which it is furnished? Intrinsic or additive? We should note that the exclusive disjunction, otherwise stated as the pure and simple option of one of the alternatives, in fact eludes the very notion of the frame, and more precisely its specific indetermination: by definition, it is never really external, nor really internal."[6]

In the context of Western art history, these are crucial but relatively arcane issues; in terms of traditional Japanese culture, such ambiguity is of the essence. For example, consider the complex and equivocal relations between interior and exterior in Japanese architecture. The covered verandah contiguous to the garden constitutes a predominantly (though not completely) exterior space when the sliding panels of the room from which it projects are closed, yet is fully continuous with the interior space when the panels—whether they be *shōji* (rice-paper partitions), *garasu-do* (glass partitions), *sugi-do* (wooden partitions), *ama-do* (wooden rain doors)—are opened or removed. These ephemeral and mobile screens are all mechanisms of the "hide and reveal" (*miegakure*) design concept—organized differently within gardens and interiors—whereby the gaze is caught in a complex play of dissimulation and revelation.

Just as the fragility of the archetypical scholar's hut, and its exposure to nature and the elements, are integral aspects of the poetic sensibility, the equivocation between outside and inside is crucial to the sense of traditional architecture. The modifiability typical of Japanese architecture by means of partitions permits an interpenetration of exterior and interior, a spatial ambiguity central to the Japanese architectural and poetic imagination. By substituting the generally round form of the plate for the normally rectangular form of the picture frame, similar considerations of equivocal framing and partitioning apply to cuisine. In Western cuisine, the effect of the plate is one of centripetal aesthetic force, so powerful that the plate itself disappears as the food is isolated and focused upon. In Japanese cuisine, the dish does not isolate the food but to the contrary connects it to the broader environment: the plate effects, as it were, a centrifugal force, such that—at least in the most successful instances—food, plate, decor, and landscape are all harmonized according to the immediate symbolism of the seasons and the subtlety of poetic allusions. In the West, the autonomy of the culinary art work is privileged; in Japan, the interdependence between dish and environment is essential.

Dishes are "compositions" in the full sense of the term, varying from *trompe l'oeil* trickery and vanitas morbidity to sheer abstraction. (The equivocation of the term "dish," meaning both the vessel and the foodstuff displayed upon it, should always be considered in its unity.) Much traditional French court and bourgeois cuisine was based on the presentation of either entire animals or recognizable parts thereof, such that the plating resembled nothing so much as a still life, particularly so for the cuisine of the hunt. In Japan, to the contrary, the use of chopsticks necessitates cutting foodstuffs into bite-size pieces, which offers totally different—and more abstract—compositional possibilities.

Consequently, Japanese culinary "iconography" differs from that of the West. It is true that stylized representations of landscape, inspired by millennia of poetic imagery, exist: a translucent paper-thin slice of white radish floating on a pool of clear broth in a black lacquer bowl set in a shadowy dining room will evoke the full moon over a pond at night, with a few sprigs of herbs laid across the orb representing reeds on the shoreline bisecting the moon. However, as with culinary illusionism in the West, these are minor effects, and the true genius of Japanese plating is its sophisticated sense of abstract composition. This was the great lesson that French chefs learned from their Japanese apprentices during that effervescent moment of the rise of the nouvelle cuisine in the 1960s and 1970s, when the French culinary establishment became increasingly open to foreign influences and when many young Japanese chefs traveled to France in order to apprentice in traditional French cuisine.

The nouvelle cuisine was a revolution not only in taste but also in style and vision. Just as important as the new techniques and foodstuffs introduced by the Japanese was a radically different manner of plating, as well as the use of an extended "tasting" menu (*menu dégustation*), both inspired by kaiseki cuisine. Perhaps the most important moment in this transformation was the publication of *Kaiseki: Zen Tastes in Japanese Cooking* (1972; the French translation, *Kaiseki: Beauté de la table au Japon*, appeared in 1973) by Tsuji Kaichi (1907–88), among the greatest modern kaiseki chefs and culinary educators.[7] This book, with its illustrations of beautifully prepared food on ceramic masterpieces, suggested to the French several hitherto more or less neglected dimensions of the culinary arts: a visual celebration of the seasons; the stress on a complex codified ordering of the meal; the multiplication of numerous small portions; and concentration on the fine details of table settings, most notably ceramics and the manner in which they are chosen to highlight the symbolism of the seasons and enhance the appearance of particular recipes. Of all these lessons, the one lost on the French concerns the profound relations between plates and plating, all the more disappointing as the great center of ceramic manufacturing in France exists at Sèvres, just outside of Paris. Nearly a half-century later we in the West are only beginning to resolve this issue.

Much can be told about a culture by the way things are composed, a word here used in the broadest sense: the arrangement of a bouquet, a dish, a photograph, a letter, a sentence, a piece of music, an outfit, a painting. Indeed, a street, a neighborhood, a city are all, ultimately, vast collective "compositions," and there exist many means of "framing" the view, not only through a camera viewfinder but also through windows, doorways, gateways, and *torii*. The placement of an object is akin to the disposition of things in a painting: a single *yuzu* fruit placed just off-center in front of a tombstone might well be sensed not just as an offering to an ancestor but also as the reorganization of the entire landscape, like the jar set upon a Tennessee hill that "made the slovenly wilderness surround that hill" in Wallace Stevens's celebrated poem "Anecdote of the Jar."[8]

In Japan, offerings in cemeteries, Buddhist temples, and Shinto shrines alike are as if "composed," sometimes according to conventional cultural symbols such as presenting a particular *kami* or local spirit its desired foods, sometimes for the most personal of reasons, like the preferred brand of whisky and cigarettes left for the posthumous pleasure of the defunct. The list of offerings is endless: the luxurious bouquets that adorn Buddhist altars, the ubiquitous rice and sake, the small piles of purificatory salt set in shrines and in front of many restaurants; also coins, incense, business cards, origami, pebbles, *mochi* (pounded rice cakes), eggs, dried fish, crustaceans, and especially fruits and vegetables of all sorts: pumpkins, watermelons, bamboo shoots, chestnuts, turnips, apples, daikon, seaweed, squash, pomegranates, persimmons—often exquisitely wrapped and beautifully arranged.[9] Just as elaborate floral offerings in Buddhist temples were among the early inspirations for ikebana, one might ask whether the vegetal offerings in Shinto shrines and Buddhist temples had in some way influenced culinary compositions.

Dōgen (1200–53), the priest, poet, and philosopher who founded the Sōtō sect of Zen, instructs the temple cook: "When cooking, do not look at ordinary things with an ordinary gaze, with ordinary feelings and thoughts. Construct a splendid abode for Buddha with the vegetable leaf that you hold between your fingers, and act so that this tiny grain of dust proclaims his Law."[10] In the Zen context, cuisine simultaneously follows moral, theological, and aesthetic imperatives. Beauty serves not only pleasure and sociability, but also enlightenment. Furthermore, in a country historically wracked by disasters of all sorts, it is apparent that the need to appease the local Shinto spirits or "holy powers," the kami, necessitates the utmost care and respect, which certainly impacts on the beauty of the offerings.

We are not passive spectators before gastronomic scenes but rather active participants, so that our degree of concentration, depth of absorption, and breadth of attention all contribute to the aesthetic effect. Just as a garden—whatever may be its compositional formula and perfection—is not like a picture, since the perspective changes with every step, a dish is also unlike its image, as its appearance changes with every bite. Unlike a painting, which always remains at a distance, in a garden we enter the work, at table the food enters us. In both cases, we need to know how to properly negotiate this encounter so as to add to, rather than diminish, the aesthetic effect and sensual pleasure.

In the culinary context, pottery variously serves as a material support, a frame that accentuates the culinary composition, a coequal part of the composition, and a dynamic element that relates to every other component of the decor.

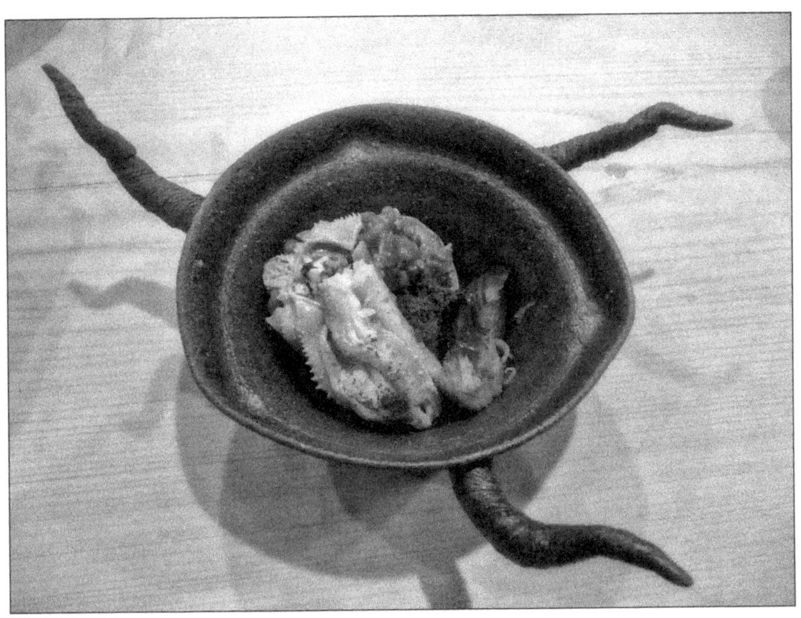

Bowl, BJR (Matsushita Ryo), Tsuzuki restaurant, Kyoto.

Consider a photograph of a seafood dish created by chef Tsuzuki Atsushi at his eponymous Kyoto restaurant Tsuzuki (minuscule, with but seven seats at the counter), featuring a bowl by the Tokoname potter known as BJR (Matsushita Ryo). At first glance, it is as if we were presented with some sort of bizarre crustacean, its carapace cut open to reveal the precise composition of its viscera. The arrangement is inseparable from the receptacle, which in turn is directly linked to the surrounding environment: the shadows of the spikes anchor the dish to the smoothly polished wooden counter, while the spikes themselves thrust outward toward both the diners and the farthest reaches of the confined space, a trace of the centrifugal force that formed the pottery on the wheel.

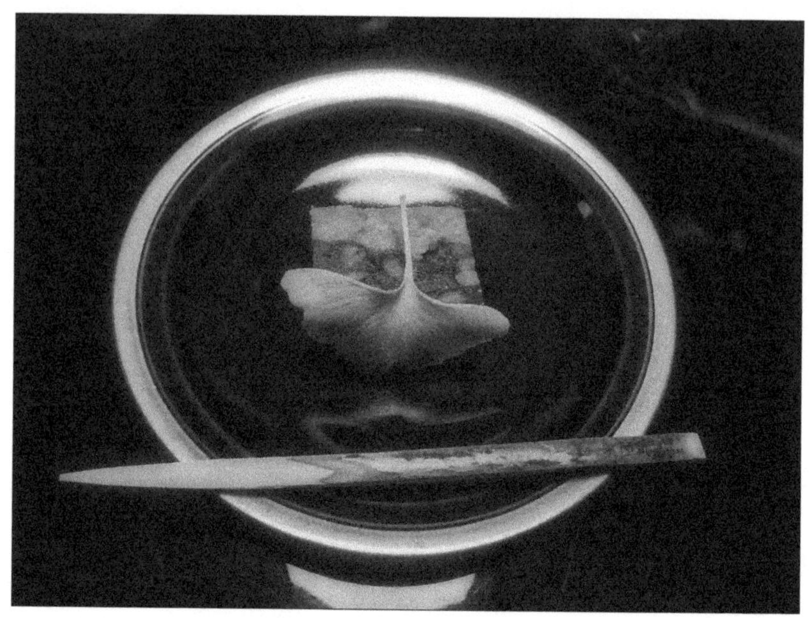

Dessert, Kikunoi Honten restaurant, Kyoto.

But soon this dynamic is reversed, as one approaches the moment of truth when the dish is to be tasted. Paying attention often means changing scale, so that when the decision must be made as to what will constitute the first bite, the scene is reduced: the spikes, indeed the dish itself, become superfluous; the room, indeed the world, disappears. How to begin? This moment of extreme centripetal attention preceding the first bite—an act of total focusing, the instant on which all gastronomy hinges—is often of the greatest ambiguity. Unlike traditional French cuisine—which is all about the blending and concentration of flavors—most kaiseki dishes instantiate what I would call a "cuisine of juxtaposition"—much in vogue in contemporary cookery worldwide—that stresses the complex contrasts between flavors, textures, and appearances. A parallel might be drawn to the different successions of wine and sake in formal dinners. Wines tend to be sequenced from less to more complex, lighter to heavier, drier to fruitier, less tannic to more tannic, and lesser to greater alcohol content. Sake, to the contrary, will be chosen by contrasts: dry against savory, floral against yeasty, cold against hot. A striking difference is that in French meals, the best wine usually comes at the climax of the meal (at which point, alas, one has often already drunk too much to appreciate the *pièce de résistance*), while according to the logic of Japanese meals, the best sake might well come first, at the moment one's palate is most receptive.

Gustatory receptivity is also at stake at the first taste of any dish. But how to begin!? This question poses two distinct problems: determining the order in which the different components of a dish should be eaten and whether they should be eaten separately or in combination, and if the latter, in precisely which conjunction. Certain aspects of a dish may hint at a solution, so that perhaps one might begin with the topmost, thus most accessible, morsel. This would make sense in Tsuzuki's dish, as the piece of crab leg is certainly the most delicate taste offered. One might hope to take solace in the belief that in Japan there is a proper way to do everything and a proper ordering of things, such as the invariable sequence of courses in kaiseki. But this suggestion is immediately frustrated by the Zen principle that hierarchies do not exist, so that no "proper" order can be determined. We are confronted with a conundrum which suggests the possibility that dining is perhaps an experimental activity.

As a foreigner, one is often in the position of not knowing what is on one's plate, and given the vast array of seafood and vegetables served in Kyoto, even my Japanese hosts are occasionally at a loss to explain what we are eating. Yet there is a far more difficult adjustment to make beyond sheer ignorance. One notable characteristic of haute cuisine is that it is generally more "refined" than other types of cuisine (peasant, familial, bourgeois), and such refinement often translates into what may be perceived as "delicateness" and "subtlety," which for some is simply sensed as blandness. The European cuisine of the hunt is an extreme case in point. The French say that the English feel a game bird is perfectly hung when the body spontaneously detaches from the neck (the English say the same about the French), but nevertheless many game lovers prefer their dishes extremely gamy. They should consequently not order game in a three-star Michelin restaurant, where such extreme flavors are rarely encountered. When Alain Senderens, one of the originators of the nouvelle cuisine, gave up his three stars at Lucas Carton, his much-quoted quip was that he wanted to be able to cook sardines.

If one prefers deeply savory, spicy, gamy foods, such restaurants would be disappointing, and this also pertains to most kaiseki establishments. One needs to adjust one's culinary palette both across cultures and within culinary hierarchies in any specific culture. I was a long-time aficionado of the great wines of Bordeaux, and my exposure to sake in the New York of the 1980s was mainly limited to inexpensive hot sake. I vividly recall the first time I tasted an excellent cold sake—a Kubota "Manju" junmai daiginjo, still among my favorites—ordered at my then favorite restaurant, the long departed Honmura-an. The very first sip was a shock, as it tasted more or less like water. (I am aware that the range of flavors of water is vast, but one needs to train one's palate to distinguish such subtle differences, just as does a wine drinker who ventures into the world of sake.) A similar situation occurred at one of the first famous restaurants where I dined in Kyoto, chef Murata Yoshihiro's Kikunoi Honten. The setting was extraordinary, the dishes among the most beautifully presented that I had ever seen, the food of a perfection typical of such establishments, and yet as I left, I felt that the entire meal was ever so slightly underwhelming, in fact somewhat bland. After years of kaiseki dining I have come to realize that the fault was with my palate, not with the cuisine, thus it was my palette that needed adjusting.

Contemporary kaiseki—for all its extravagence and luxuriousness—still bears something of the understated elegant rusticity central to the wabi-sabi aesthetic from which it arose. Culinary scholar Ryoko Sekiguchi explains that the principles of Japanese cuisine are founded on "an aesthetic of delicateness," and that in particular the cuisine of Kyoto is reputed to be, "*usuaji*, literally: 'pale tasting.'"[11] An untrained palate confronted with a particularly subtle cuisine can hardly be discriminating. Emblematic of my coming to terms with this cuisine is that it is in Japan where for the first time in my life I have come to appreciate white bread: not only because of the high quality of the product but because I have become attuned to a degree of subtlety and, I might say quite bluntly, of blandness greater than that which I had previously been capable of appreciating. A slice of thick lightly toasted white bread, spread thinly with yuzu preserves, served with *genmaicha* (green tea with roasted brown rice), makes for an ideal breakfast.

There is yet one more important factor, derived from tea aesthetics, in this gastronomic dynamic: the sense of aesthetic complicity between host and guest, between restaurateur and client. For an aliment, object, or edifice is fundamentally a nexus of social relations. At home, we try our best to set a table and serve a meal in accord with the predilections—and even the culinary and aesthetic erudition (not to mention the limitations)—of our guests. This is of course much more difficult to accomplish in a restaurant, where the table setting and menu are generally decided in advance and imposed upon the diner. However, the tiny scale of so many restaurants in Japan, as well as the great exclusivity of many of them—where occasionally it is difficult to get a reservation without already being a client, or at least getting a recommendation from one—permits such aesthetic collusion. In a fine Western restaurant the maître d'hôtel might make note of the table one prefers, the type of martini that is desired, and the appropriate moment that this cocktail be brought to the table, while in Japan the chef might well remember one's favorite potter and compose the platings of an entire meal accordingly.[12] Furthermore, if a regular returns to a kaiseki restaurant twice in the same week, most probably the chef will compose a special menu for that person alone so as not to repeat dishes from the previous visit.

Yet there are also simple gestures, applicable even to total strangers, that personalize a meal. For example, upon ordering sake one is often presented with a tray full of sake cups (*guinomi, ochoko, sakazuki*) from which to choose, and occasionally the cup, as well as the flask (*tokkuri*), is changed as each new sake arrives, such that the change of cup harmonizes with the change of sake. The guest would ideally use the same criteria in choosing a cup that the host or chef uses in selecting the rest of the tableware, following all the complexities that govern Japanese culinary and ceramic aesthetics. There are more idiosyncratic examples. I once gave

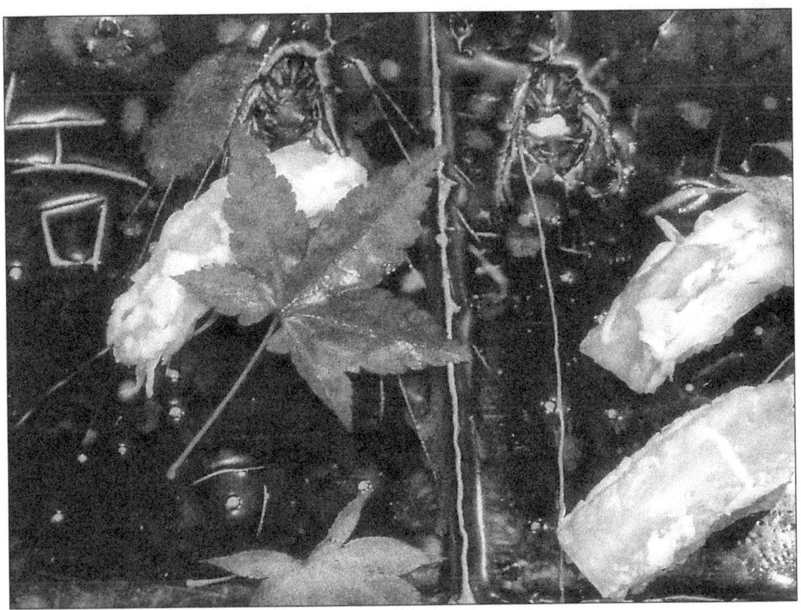

Sushi on ceramic plate with cicada imprint, Koie Ryōji, Ifuki restaurant, Kyoto.

as a gift to my tea and pottery friends Umeda Mitsuko and Umeda Minoru a small ceramic cicada—an insect so important in Japanese seasonal symbolism—found in the market at Nice. Unbeknownst to me, they lent it to potter Koie Ryōji, whose work I collect. He used it to make imprints on a large pottery platter, which was acquired by the Kyoto restaurant Ifuki. One dinner there with the Umedas featured the ceramics of Koie, and when the fish course arrived, I was surprised to find my tray upside down—placed that way to reveal the cicada imprints.

This situational gastronomic aesthetic is beautifully expressed by the great poet and traveler Matsuo Bashō (1644–94) in his account of a trip to Sarashina, where he is lodged in the home of a poor priest. As the priest recounts his own journeys, Bashō notices that—in a passage that

Tanizaki must have known by heart before writing *In Praise of Shadows*—"moonlight poured through leaves and cracks in the wall into a corner of the room."[13] Bashō falls into a melancholic mood, revealing that "my heart and mind felt the utter aloneness of autumn," and the reader anticipates that the poet will continue with expected expressions of mono no aware. However, quite the opposite occurs: "I suggested we have a drink in the moonlight, and our host quickly brought cups. Too large for refined tastes, they were trimmed with gaudy gold lacquer. City sophisticates wouldn't have touched them. But finding them in the back country, they pleased me. They were, I thought, more precious than the blue jeweled cups of the wealthy."[14] The situation would seem to warrant cups that harmonize with the understated and rustic wabi-sabi aesthetic, but the charm of Bashō is often his flouting of convention, which increases the poignancy of the moment. The poem that immediately follows stresses this hyperbolic and somewhat comical reversal of customary usage:

> *I'd sprinkle lacquer,*
> *a decorative picture*
> *on this hotel moon.*[15]

It is generally the moon's light that renders precious and mysterious all that it touches, but here the glow of the cheap lacquer—contrary to expectations, and in testimony to the priest's unaffected gesture—increases the beauty of that most beautiful of images, the moon. I imagine that Bashō, like so many before and after him, drank the reflection of the moon itself as he downed the sake in that glimmering lacquer cup.

4

Untimely Moons

THE GARDEN

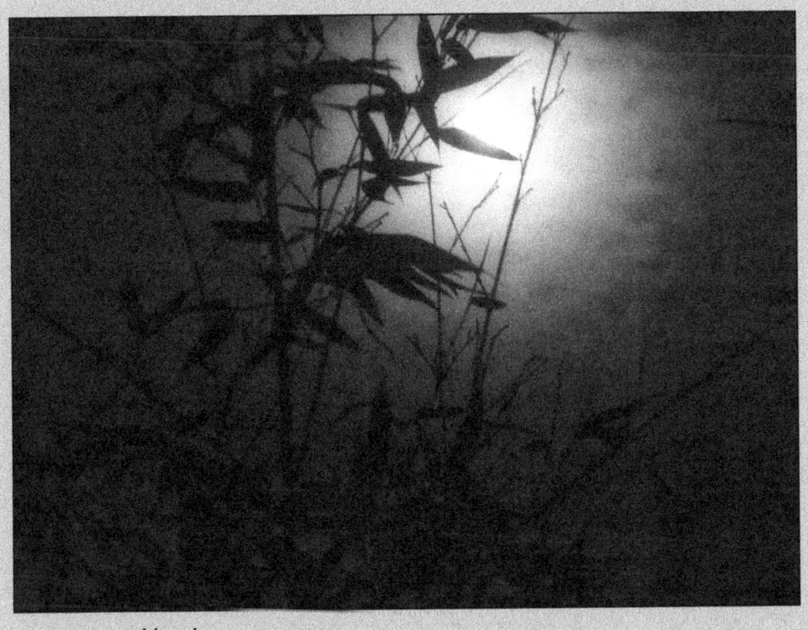

Moon and bamboo.

Before leaving Paris for Kyoto in late autumn 2015, I decided to "compose" a gift that would be a rebus for a much-awaited moment. At the Paris shop Mariage Frères, whose teas are greatly appreciated in Japan, I purchased several packages apiece of their "Pleine Lune" (Full Moon) and "Noël" (Christmas) teas. In the Japanese tea ceremony, all objects are carefully chosen to suggest a seasonal theme, and an integral aspect of the event is the decoding of these signs. Once, at a tea ceremony at Kōzan-ji temple in the mountains northwest of Kyoto the day after a lunar eclipse, I discovered that the scroll in the tokonoma bore the calligraphic inscription of the *kanji* (Chinese ideograms adapted for the Japanese language) for "darkness," while the ceramic incense burner by Fukumoto Fuku represented a silver crescent moon. Such attention to metaphor is greatly appreciated, so though the particular teas I chose in France could not be used in the tea ceremony, I thought that at least the puzzle—its solution being that this year the first full moon of winter would fall on Christmas—would amuse my friends. Gift-giving is a very serious activity in Japan, with elaborate formalized protocols concerning the wrapping, presentation, and every other aspect of the activity, differing according to the recipient and the occasion. This is so complex that some families even have a member who serves the role of designated gift specialist. Alas, only one person who received this gift rebus solved the riddle, Umeda Mitsuko (mentioned earlier regarding the gold-lacquered fish bone).

On that Christmas evening, I went to one of my

favorite places in Kyoto—the west bank at the confluence of the Kamo and Takano rivers at Demachiyanagi, the spot that marks the beginning of the sacred space leading to the Shimogamo shrine—to await the rise of the full moon over the Higashiyama mountains. The philosopher and theologian D. T. Suzuki reminds us of the importance of the moon in Japanese culture: "The moonlight singularly attracts the Japanese imagination, and any Japanese who ever aspired to compose a waka or a haiku would hardly dare leave the moon out [. . .] The moonlight is illuminating enough, but owing to the atmospheric conditions all objects under it appear not too strongly individualized; a certain mystic obscurantism pervades."[1]

Anybody who has read an anthology of haiku immediately notes that the moon is among the most important poetic images—along with plum and cherry blossoms, red maple leaves, and pine trees—a realization confirmed by even the most casual perusal of Japanese woodblocks, paintings, and decorative arts. There even exist moon-viewing platforms attached to temples, palaces, and private residences, where the perfect viewpoint is established for contemplating the perfect moon, preferably with a glass of sake in hand, within which appears the moon's unstable and ephemeral double. (When Bruno Taut saw one such platform at the Katsura Detached Palace, he was moved nearly to tears.) The term moonstruck or moondrunk is brought to new aesthetic levels. In *The Dharma Bums*, Jack Kerouac has the narrator, inspired by the Zen Buddhism of Gary Snyder, describe an extraordinary nocturnal experience at his remote mountain lookout on Desolation Peak in the North Cascades Mountain Range in the state of Washington: "When I went back in the moonlight to my same old tree stump the world was like a dream, like a phantom, like a bubble, like a shadow, like a vanishing dew, like a lightning flash."[2] Each simile in this enumeration is a classic image of the ephemeral nature of existence, and the very hybridity of the list mixes commonplaces of both Japanese *mono no aware* and Western *vanitas*, appropriate to a poet like Snyder, whose life has been dedicated to the meeting of East and West.

The spot I chose on the river is particularly beloved, and during major seasonal events such as *sakura* (cherry blossom) viewing, the crowds are notoriously huge. Awaiting moonrise, I remembered the warning of Murasaki Shikibu (c. 973 or 978–c. 1014 or 1031), author of *The Tale of Genji*: "People say that it is dangerous to look at the moon in solitude." But just like this great writer, I felt that "something impels me, and sitting a little withdrawn I muse there."[3] I knew that officially moonrise would be just before five o'clock in the early evening, but that the moon would actually appear somewhat later due to the time it would take to rise over the low eastern mountains. So I arrived well in advance to settle onto my favorite bench and was rather surprised to find nobody there. Perhaps everyone awaited the last moment, since the timing was so easily calculable. Finally, still alone, I saw the first glimmer of light on the horizon. The globe ascended behind the peaks, to briefly balance itself upon the mountaintop before entering the urban realm. A cyclist quickly passed by, without turning his head. Another did the same. I was still alone, in this most popular of spots.

The full moon was indeed beautiful, seen above the leafless branches of the willows (*yanagi*) for which this district, Demachiyanagi, is named. But I finally realized that it was—if not for me, certainly for the rest of the populace—*the*

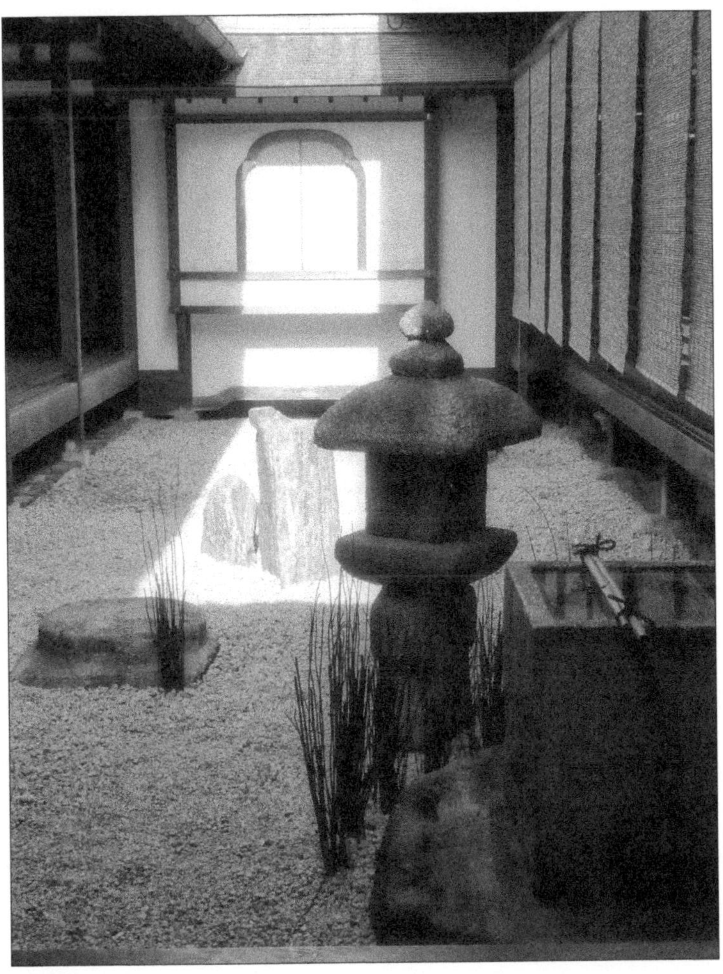

Zuihō-in.

wrong moon! For while I was experiencing the first winter moon—what in America is sometimes referred to as the "cold moon"—the poets, painters, and moon-lovers of Japan are enamored almost exclusively of the "harvest moon" of early autumn. I should have known better, since Yoshida Kenkō (1283–1350), in his classic *Essays in Idleness* (1330–32), proclaims of the winter moon: "There is something forlorn about the waning winter moon, shining cold and clear in the sky, unwatched because it is said to be depressing."[4] Centuries earlier, in her autobiography, Murasaki Shikibu exclaimed: "Yet, perhaps because I still retain the conviction that I am not the kind of person to abandon herself completely to despair, on autumn evenings, when nostalgia is at its most poignant, I go out and sit on the verandah to gaze in reverie. 'Is this the moon that used to praise my beauty?' I say to myself, as I conjure up memories of the past."[5] The English translator of this work reminds us of "a belief that it was dangerous for a woman to look at the moon too often; it promoted nostalgia, grief, and hence premature aging."[6] One must carefully choose one's moon, and different moons demand different rituals in different cultures. This early winter moon was no less beautiful than the autumn moon, but in Kyoto it was less significant, indeed insignificant. This led me to realize that concerning my gift rebus, perhaps I should have remembered that at Christmas one evokes the star of Bethlehem, not the moon.

Zen gardens

In his essay "On Exile," the renowned Greek-Roman biographer, essayist, magistrate, and Delphic priest Plutarch (46–120 CE) famously mocked those who claimed that the Athenian moon is more beautiful than the Corinthian moon. He might be right in doing so, but it could be argued that the Japanese moon is the most beautiful of all, not because of anything that may be confirmed with a telescope but rather due to its profound poetic and literary history. One might also say the same for certain types of trees and flowers, even for rain, mist, and fog. The novelist Kawabata Yasunari (1899–1972), in the preface to a book by the landscape painter Higashiyama Kaii (1908–99), recounts his reaction to having seen the famous Three Pines at Kanazawa, one of the great natural sites of Japan, celebrated in painting and poetry through the ages: "They struck me to the point that I wondered if there existed a comparable beauty anywhere in the world. I was overwhelmed with thanks for that state of mind among the Japanese that would not hesitate to consecrate centuries to transmitting the beauty of a single tree."[7] In reading this, we need imagine all those famous places (*meisho*), things, and even sounds transformed into poetry and imagery, all destined to devolve into commonplaces: the "three most scenic places" (Miyajima, Amanohashidate, Matsushima), the "three most beautiful gardens" (Kenroku-en, Koraku-en, Kairaku-en), the Fifty-three Stations of the Tōkaidō, the Thirty-six Views of Mount Fuji, the Hundred Famous Views of Edo, and so forth.

We both see and *see according to* a work of art, and much the same may be said for nature, which not only constantly reveals its ever-changing beauty but also teaches us—as objects vary in changing light, sundry meteorological conditions, and seasonal transformations—how to employ its forms and their metamorphoses. Every aspect of nature evokes specific emotions and poetic allusions, as geographer and Japan specialist Augustin Berque explains: "Rain, for example, is quite other than a mere precipitation of water (its objective form). A certain rain will only fall during a certain season, or even at a specific moment of the day, because it is inseparable from an entire world of sensations,

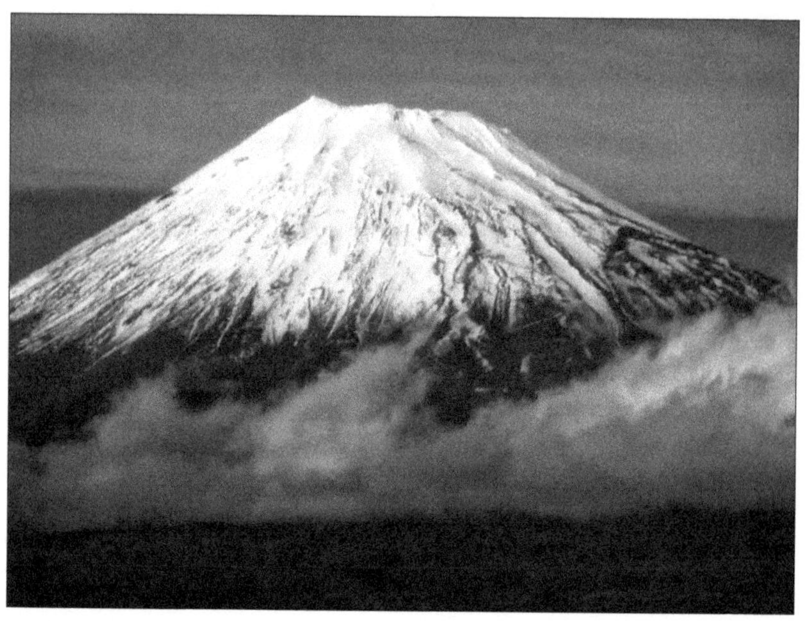

Mount Fuji.

emotions, and evocations whose more or less codified associations relate it to a certain landscape."[8] And of course, not only do different sorts of rain evoke different emotions and allusions but they also, like the light of the moon, attenuate visibility so as to create an ambiance of vagueness and suggestiveness. A "poetic" ambiance, one might say.

While Western philosophy radically separates particular objects and ideal forms, artists East and West can, as if by magic, make of the particular an ideal, a veritable archetype. This might appear to occur with the mere spontaneous stroke of a brush, yet as with any craft, a proper brushstroke is prepared by countless gestures repeated over a lifetime, indeed over centuries of acquired tradition. It is often said that it takes ten thousand hours of practice to become adept at a craft: the sushi apprentice doesn't touch any rice for two years, much less prepare the fish; it takes ten years for a Bunraku puppeteer to master the movement of just the marionette's left arm; forty years normally pass before the potter may reach artistic maturity, or before the tea master can begin to imagine creating an individual style. As Ezra Pound and the famed Japan scholar Ernest Fenollosa exclaim of Noh theater, ". . . the poet may even be silent while gestures consecrated by four centuries of usage show meaning."[9]

For the traditional Japanese arts, there is always a *proper* way of doing things. This might seem exasperatingly limiting to Westerners imbued with the ideology of freedom and creativity in their everyday and aesthetic existence, but such codes of propriety guarantee an extraordinary level of technical and performative proficiency, and permit a comprehensive grasp of forms and functions, making of craft a means of meditation and of spectatorship a type of erudition. Landscape architect David A. Slawson opens his book *Secret Teachings in the Art of Japanese Gardens* with an anecdote to this effect. One day he assisted in the year-end cleaning of the gardens at the Yabunouchi tea school in Kyoto. He had been working Japanese style, squatting with both feet planted firmly on the ground. At one point, to relieve the tension, he shifted his weight to the ball of one foot and was immediately reprimanded by the crew chief, who explained that by doing so he destroyed the harmony of the garden.[10] In a culture where one may gain enlightenment through the sweeping of a path, such ungainliness is no mean thing. For to be "cultured" is to realize that a gesture is always a symbol. One need *respect* the spirit of a place, and one must obviously also *see* according to that spirit. Such is the responsibility of the visitor.

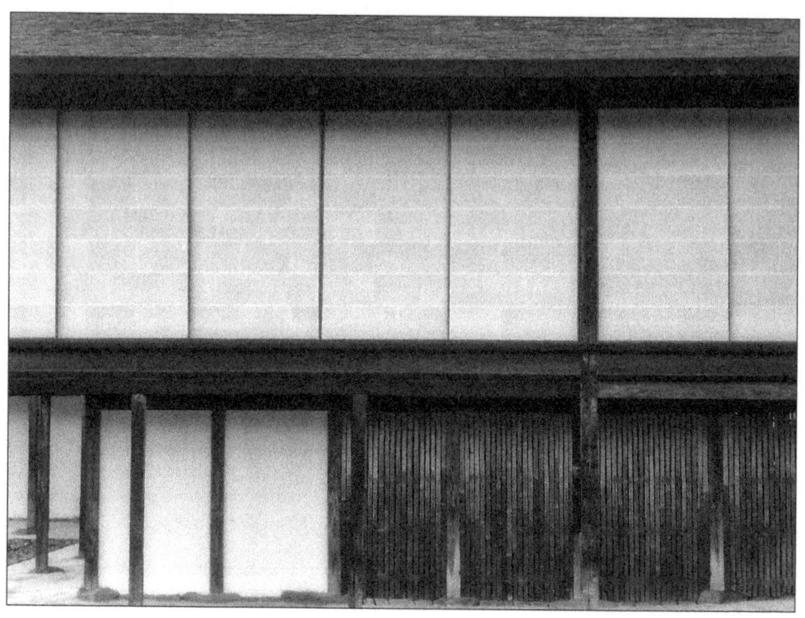

Katsura Detached Palace.

It is often asked why Japanese-style "dry" or "Zen" gardens are so rarely convincing outside of Japan. Beautiful, perhaps, but somehow not quite "authentic." Most immediately, one could point to the many material differences between Japanese and Western gardens. First of all, vegetation differs, and even the most subtle substitutions produce a different sense of place; traditional construction techniques diverge, something that is apparent at even the most cursory glance at enclosures; fence styles, with their very specific use of certain types of bamboo and elaborate knot-tying techniques, are totally dissimilar (there exist at least 150 different styles of such fencing in Kyoto); and of course the entirety of the adjacent architecture has little in common with Japanese types, from the largest forms to the tiniest details.

Furthermore, psychologically ingrained forms of Western spatial organization—such as the pictorially based perspectival projections that structure such "formal" gardens as Vaux-le-Vicomte and Versailles—do not coincide with the gaze, posture, and gestures demanded by a Japanese garden. Perhaps even more important is the manner in which the modularity of the tatami floor mats and the *fusuma* (sliding interior panels)—generally of the same size, thus establishing congruence of proportion between horizontal and vertical dimensions—relates to interiors, architecture, and gardens alike. All traditional architectural measurements are based upon a single unit, the *ken* (approximately two meters), the distance across two structural columns. The standard measure of surface area (like our square foot or square meter) is the *tsubo* (one square ken, the equivalent of two tatami placed together to form a square). Tatami exist in a standard size (the three major versions, of Kyoto, Tokyo, and Nagoya, have nearly identical dimensions)—one ken long and one-half ken wide—and the space of interiors is calculated according to the number of tatami; thus one would speak of a "six-mat room" or an "eight-mat room."

This standard modularity creates a fundamental sense of proportion not unlike that of the golden rectangle in Western art, but vastly more widespread, indeed ubiquitous. (In the West, we calculate in square feet or square meters, but these are abstract, not concrete, dimensions and we do not generally *see* according to these measurements. To speak of a thirty-square-meter room gives a sense of size, but not shape or proportion.) And since such proportions obtain in both the vertical and horizontal dimensions, they also inflect the sense in which architecture frames the surroundings.

The tatami thus articulates interior and exterior, architecture and landscape. It is a fundamental element of everyday life, all the more so since one sits directly upon the tatami—engaging the sense of touch, thus making architecture all the more intimate—such that this spatial module is psychologically interiorized, in size and proportion as well as in relation to gesture and vision. Since sitting also has its proper form in Japan—the formal *seiza* position—body posture is as ritualized, one might even say choreographed, as everything else. Thus the very existence of tatami, as well as our manner of sitting on them, will transform the experience of house and garden. (Truth be told, for most Westerners, and an increasing number of Japanese, this form of sitting is all but impossible, more an excruciating distraction than a path to enlightenment, to the extent that in contemporary Japan, seiza slips from the real to the ideal. The experience of architecture and design has certainly followed.)

Perhaps the crucial factor in the distinctiveness of the Japanese garden is the amazing attention paid to craftsmanship and the extraordinary level of care afforded these gardens, derived from ancient and profound Shinto concerns with purity and Buddhist rituals of cleanliness. In many such temples, one of the main jobs of novices is tending the gardens. I have often, for example, seen gardeners in Kyoto crouching, nose to the ground, using tweezers to remove the first minuscule shoots of weeds sprouting amidst huge expanses of moss. One anecdote will suffice. The garden of Kenroku-en in Kanazawa, one of the "Three Great Gardens of Japan"—where the great pines are protected, branch by branch, with elaborate rope systems to support them against the heavy winter snows—has a stream running

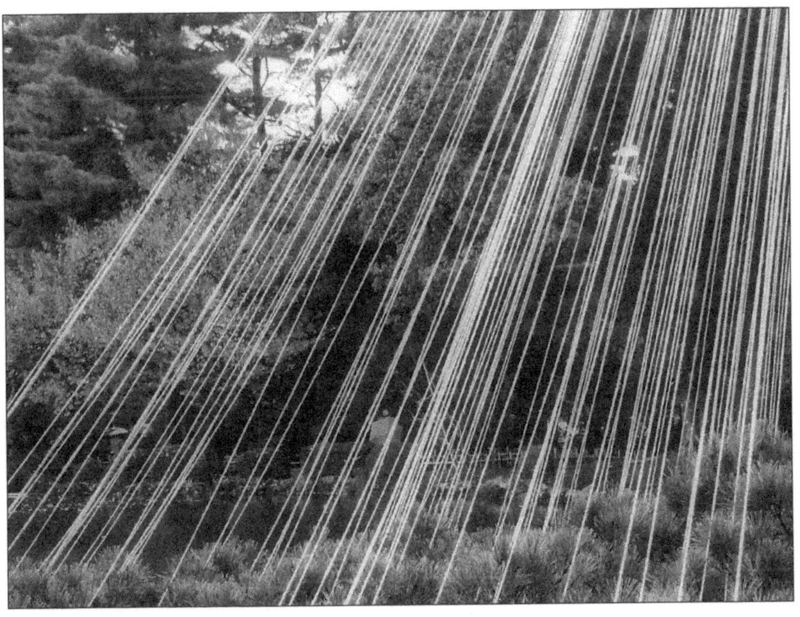

Kenroku-en garden, Kanazawa.

through it. One day I saw a group of men in high rubber boots advancing in two rows: the first five men were clearly skimming fallen leaves off the water, but it was unclear what the others in the second row were doing, as their instruments were under water. When asked, they explained that they were sweeping the stones at the bottom of the water. They bemoaned the fact that these days it is difficult to get enough help, for in previous times the workers would remove each and every stone from the stream so as to thoroughly clean them one by one, to then carefully set them back in their proper place!

Finally, the Japanese garden, especially of the *karesansui* type (the term for what we call the dry or Zen garden, literally: "dry mountain water"), remains a symbolic space, a

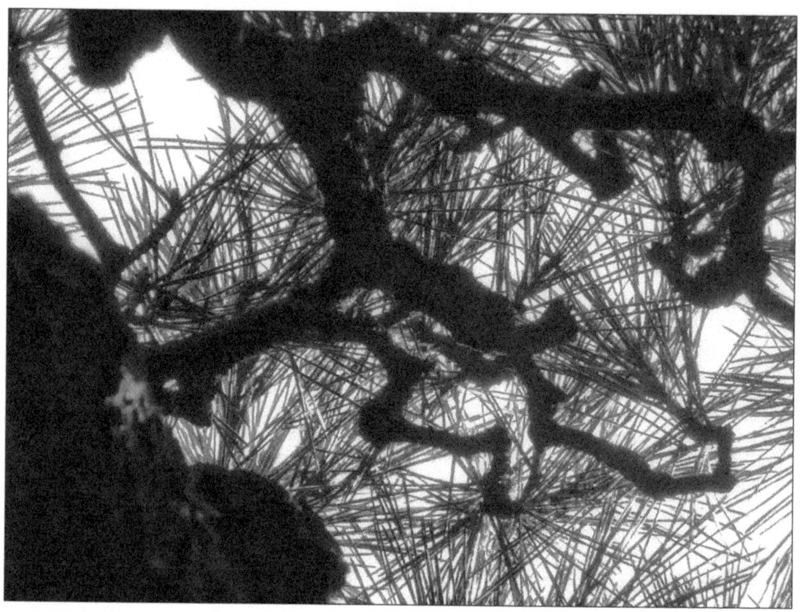

Ritsurin garden, Takamatsu.

vast condensation of nature into a minuscule space. A single lantern covered in moss may represent an entire forest floor, a single stone a mountain, some gravel the ocean. Here, remarkable natural forms permeate poetic vision; proper pruning follows. Needless to say, in Japan pruning is traditionally done according to strict rules. One learns by looking at nature, and one learns how to look at nature by looking at drawings, which were sketched by looking at nature—such is what we call tradition, though a more technical word for the process would be stylization, if not mannerism. Gardeners might consult a work like the 15th-century classic by Zōen, *Illustrations for Designing Mountain, Water, and Hillside Field Landscapes*, while poets might contemplate drawings by the great Chinese literati painters and their Japanese successors, such as Tenshō Shūbun (1444–50) and Sesshū Tōyō (c. 1420–1506). Landscaping, painting, and poetry intertwine in a long but coherent and relatively stable iconographic tradition: poets will write of the strength and longevity of tormented pines, painters will depict these same pines to accentuate these characteristics, and gardeners will consequently reproduce them by careful planting and pruning. There are thus proper ways to paint pines and proper ways to trim pines, and the two greatly resemble each other.

It is through generous poetic license that we can speak of such imagery as "natural." A modern anecdote is revealing. It is told that one day a Japanese gardener visited a Swiss friend at his estate in Switzerland. On the property were several spectacular ancient pines, and as a surprise gift, one day during the proprietor's absence the gardener pruned them to perfection—*Japanese* perfection. The Swiss friend returned to find his beloved trees totally mutilated! The conceit in Japanese gardening and flower arranging is to make the garden or bouquet look "natural," though the results are often idealized and formalized to the point that it would be quite difficult to make something that *less* resembles the natural environment. In seeking to transport, transpose, and condense nature, the landscaper or ikebana artist creates something metaphoric, symbolic, emblematic; something more "natural" than nature itself: idealized nature, what today we with a different eye might speak of in terms of hyperreality, or sometimes even surreality.

The preferred beauties of nature derive from a centuries-old amalgam of animist, Shinto, and Buddhist interactions with the environment, inflected by those Chinese pictorial traditions (principally of the Southern Song

Dynasty) later emulated by Japanese poets and artists, many of whom were Zen monks. Art transfigured the landscape in purporting to imitate nature, then tradition turned such imagery, both poetic and pictorial, into the emblems, paradigms, and commonplaces according to which subsequent generations would view nature.

This is less obviously but equally true for the sounds of the natural world. In the West we certainly hear the sea in Claude Debussy's *La mer*, where we can sense the onset of a squall and the calm that follows; we may even be able to identify many of the birds in Olivier Messiaen's *Catalogue d'oiseaux*. Yet it would be impossible to distinguish between the various pines (at the Villa Borghese, the Janiculum, the Appian Way, and near a catacomb) in Ottorino Respighi's composition *Pines of Rome*, or even imagine that we were listening to the wind coursing through any pines whatsoever.[11]

In Japan, these allusions are highly conventionalized, and if a poem evokes the sound of the wind, chances are that it will be the soughing of the wind in the pines. Indeed, one Japanese maxim proclaims that "inhaling all the wind in the pine trees, the soul is never soiled."[12] We are attuned to this sound and listen for it at appropriate moments, so it becomes all the more easy to hear it, for example, in one of the most famous works for shakuhachi flute, *Matsukaze* (Wind in the Pines). Notwithstanding the fact that the shakuhachi is the instrument that sounds most like the wind, this sonic trope is widespread: Okakura Kakuzō describes, in *The Book of Tea*, the sonic ambiance of a tea ceremony: "The kettle sings well, for pieces of iron are so arranged in the bottom as to produce a peculiar melody in which one may hear the echoes of a cataract muffled by clouds, of a distant sea breaking among the rocks, a rainstorm sweeping

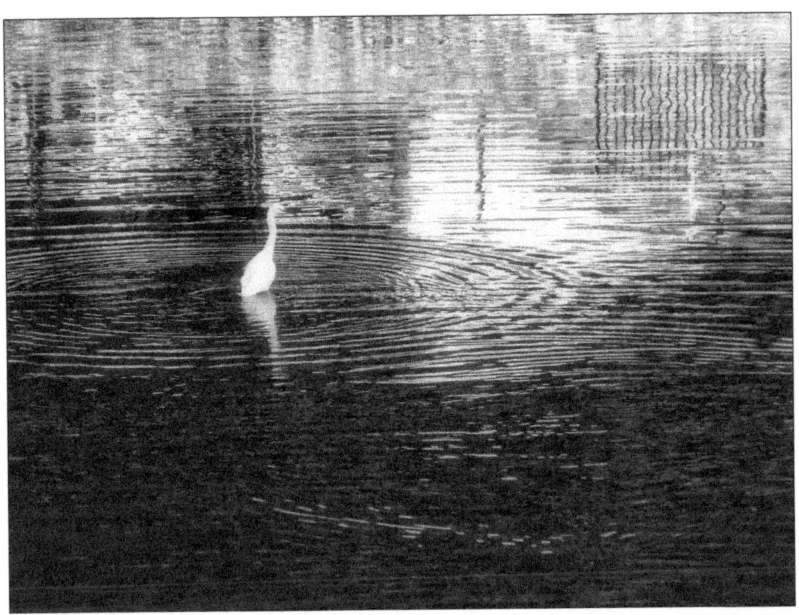

Heron in the Takano River, Kyoto.

through a bamboo forest, or of the soughing of pines on some faraway hill."[13] I, for one, would also love to celebrate the distinctive and mysterious sound of the wind in a bamboo grove—with its whistling glissandi punctuated by the "clacks" of the bamboo striking each other—but that would be like contemplating the December moon.

Different species of trees in different types of forests make different sorts of sounds in the wind, and some observers, like Thoreau or the German writer, folklorist, composer, and great wanderer in the German landscape, Hans Jürgen von der Wense, can indeed hear these differences, as the latter proclaims: "To differentiate the trees by their sounds, to recognize the eight winds by their melodies."[14] He goes further, to reveal that certain European traditions outside the mainstream do indeed have a subtle ear for the musicality of the natural world: "Each thing on earth has its divine inner melody. I know shaman songs from the Laplanders of Finland, who give a melody to every brook, every mountain, every flower, and every cloud—a kind of musical inventory or archive of nature."[15] This is not unlike the manner in which in Japan every natural object might enshrine a kami. However, we in the West generally do not have musical, poetic, or literary traditions that much care for such subtle distinctions, even given acute hearing and perfect pitch, and despite the fact that much music is composed for those Western instruments capable of quite subtle imitations of nature. We should attend to the clues about how to listen and what to listen for, all the while paying attention to the forms and limits of sonic representation.

However, at times the acceleration of modernization produces catastrophic results. I walk the paths of Daitoku-ji—that temple complex where the wabi-sabi tea ceremony was perfected, and where so much of the great art of Kyoto is still to be found—not intent on visiting any particular subtemple this day but just to have the pleasure of quietude among the fabulous trees. There is wind among the pines. All of a sudden, the artificial squall of a gas-powered leaf blower blasts the air.

Atmospheric aesthetics

I have long wished to organize a museum exhibition entitled *Atmosphere*. It would not be centered on immateriality (*Les Immatérieux*, Centre Pompidou, 1985), or on pure color (*Azur*, Fondation Cartier, 1993), nor would it be a study of formlessness (*L'Informe*, Centre Pompidou, 1996), but rather an investigation of the borderline between figuration and abstraction, of the point at which objects disappear into or emerge from smoke and smog, fog and mist. Even more fundamentally, it would examine the iconographic instability between figure and ground, and the ambiguous relationship that links material surface and visual illusion.[16]

In *Glimpses of Unfamiliar Japan*, Lafcadio Hearn recounts a tale about Kōbō Daishi (Kūkai), legendary calligrapher and founder of the Shingon sect of Buddhism. One day he was sitting on a riverbank and a small boy came up to him to ask if he was really Kōbō Daishi. He confirmed his identity, but doubting the reply, the boy challenged him to write on the sky, something he immediately did. During the turbulent decade of the 1960s, the painter and sculptor Jules Olitski suggested an act of elegant aesthetic provocation, extraordinary in its simplicity and profound in its ramifications. He claimed that the ideal work of art would be to spray the air with a can of aerosol paint such that the color would remain suspended for a certain amount of time, an ephemeral three-dimensional Olitski in the sky.[17] The breeze would make of this painting a kinetic sculpture, or a quasi-cinematographic abstraction. It would then disappear, a total dematerialization of the art work. This fantasy evokes the ambiguities and hybridizations of the arts in 1960s New York: simultaneously proto-cinema and performance art, pastiche of action painting and avatar of minimalism. The mutable and evanescent results of Olitski's gesture highlight the role of the transient in art, as the dissipating colored cloud, a fragile and ephemeral presence, vanishes into thin air. However briefly, the atmosphere is revealed as both subject and medium, figure and ground, drawing and support. We realize that pure transparency is tantamount

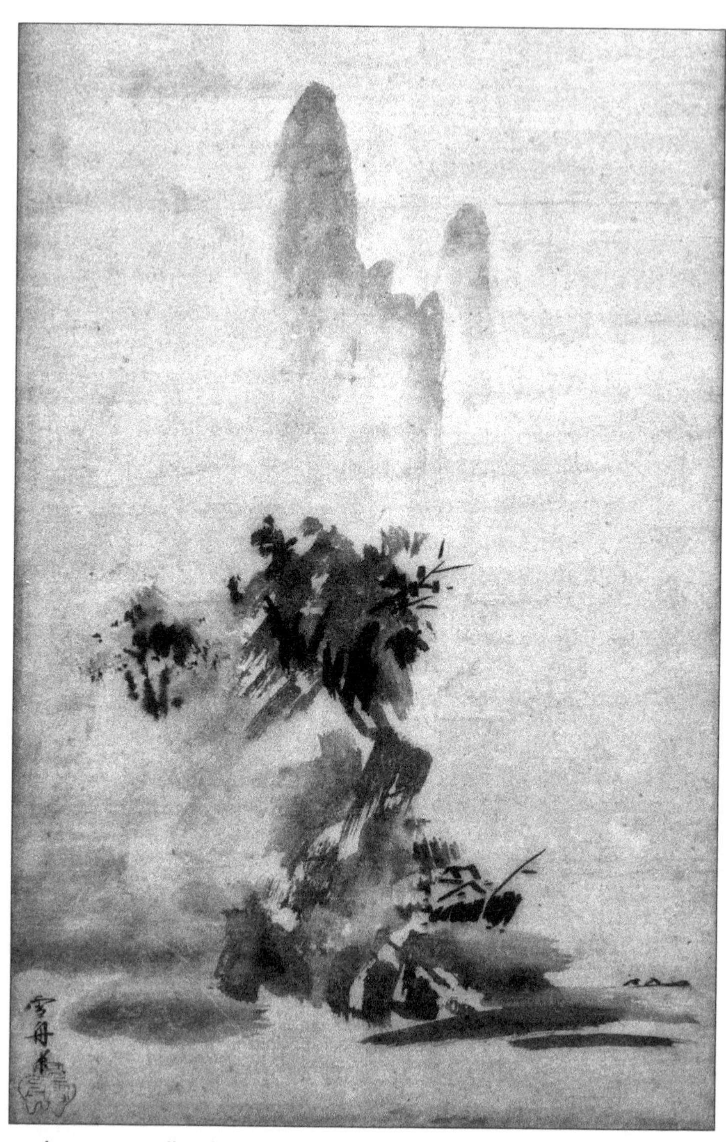

Sesshū Tōyō, scroll (ink on paper, 1495).

to invisibility, and that visibility is ambiguous, a function of both translucency and opacity. When the ether is troubled, it becomes atmosphere, a veritable labyrinth of vision. Olitski's gesture is emblematic of his entire oeuvre, often characterized as atmospheric blankets of colored spray; it could also serve as an emblem of the exhibition *Atmosphere*.

During the half millennium since the European Renaissance, the notion of *atmosphere* has suggested the very essence of transparency, or at least translucency. The evolution of optical and representational techniques privileged the clear and distinct forms of linear perspective to the detriment of atmospheric effects. Canvas, page, and atmospheric interferences disappear to permit the image to appear. Perfected by Leonardo da Vinci, "atmospheric perspective"—which might well have contained diverse effects—was reduced to its most impoverished form: the loss of detail in the distance, occasionally enhanced by a faint haze and a bluish tinge. For the most part, the atmosphere became invisible, cleansed of all imperfections, and pictorial transparency was emblematized by a realm of objects such as window panes, glassware, and bubbles, signs of painterly virtuosity and worldly vanity.

Lafcadio Hearn describes how, to the contrary, Japanese artists had long succeeded in revealing the astonishingly transformative effects of atmosphere on the landscape: "Yet these Oriental landscapes possess charms of colour extraordinary, phantom-colour delicate, elfish, indescribable—created by the wonderful atmosphere. Vapours enchant the distances, bathing peaks in bewitchments of blue and grey of a hundred tones, transforming naked cliffs to amethyst, stretching spectral gauzes across the topazine morning, magnifying the splendour of noon by effacing the

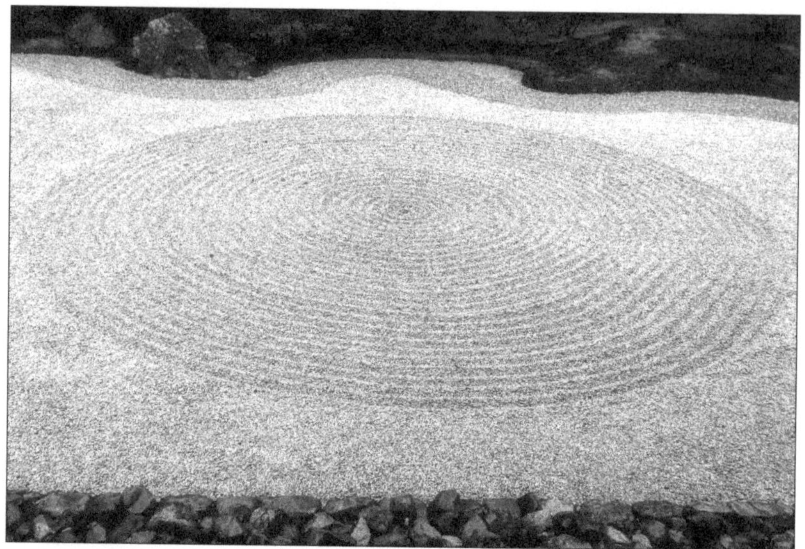

Kennin-ji.

horizon, filling the evening with smoke of gold, bronzing the waters, banding the sundown with ghostly purple and green of nacre."[18] We see such enchanting visions perfected by a painter like James Abbott McNeill Whistler.

Film theorist Annette Michelson evokes Olitski's gesture as she recounts an amusing tale of trying to choose the cover image for an exhibition on experimental film. A friend suggested that she use the shot of an empty film frame, or a screen without image, to which she replied: "But then, whose frame or screen is it to be? To which film-maker do I go, to Brakhage, Snow, Jacobs, or Frampton? To Breer, Mekas, Kubelka, Sharits?"[19] This was written in 1978, at the peak moment of the theoretical concern with the material specificity of the art work: the wealth of iconoclastic richness revealed by Michelson's anecdote was meant to stress the fundamental equivocation between film projection as event, image as illusion, and screen as object. We were already deep into an epoch where silence, the blank page, the white canvas, the empty screen, and the vacant gallery signaled a crisis of the art object, so it should not be surprising to find more than a hint of Zen in so many works of this epoch. However, the iconographic ambiguity of emptiness had been an issue in Western art for centuries, at least as early as Baroque painting, where the pure transparency of the cloudless azure sky evinced a form of dematerialization, an imagination without images that reaches toward infinity, toward the very incommensurability of God. The metaphysical declension from blueness to discoloration to infinite depth to void is an instance of iconoclasm at the very core of the image, serving as an unfathomable symbol of transcendence. It results in what philosopher Gaston Bachelard writes of as an "absolute intimate sublimation."[20]

In Asia, the situation is quite the opposite. The theory and practice of painting and drawing in Southern Song Dynasty China—a golden age of Chinese painting, which was to become a major influence on Japanese art—celebrated the myriad effects of indistinctness, incompleteness, suggestiveness, allusion. Here, the material corollate of atmosphere is the white canvas or page. In China and Japan, not only do calligraphy and ink drawing share the same page or scroll, but they are at times nearly indistinguishable, since the freely formed cursive or "grass" script may suggest imagery, and in any case the shape of the ubiquitous painted bamboo leaf closely resembles that of a modulated calligraphic brushstroke. The ambiguity of the image is complicated by the heterogeneity of the surface, as the white background of page or scroll variously appears as material support or representational space, depending upon the disposition of the writing and drawing. It may represent haze, fog, mist, snow, sky, or just pure depth, often indistinguishable from each other. Thus whiteness (what Japanese painters call *yohaku*, blank space or leftover white) may be background or foreground, figuration or decoration, earthly or celestial. It is here that perspective and atmosphere at times combine to suggest the inexpressible feeling of Zen emptiness: to be well practiced in seeing the fullness of the world on the emptiness of the paper, or the emptiness of paper as emblematic of spiritual fulfillment.

Such equivocation between abstraction and figuration also exists regarding non-linguistic traces and calligraphy, as artist and critic Takiguchi Shūzō explains: "we naturally look for signs within what at a glance appear to be automatic and abstract lines."[21] Every kanji necessitates a determinate number of brushstrokes, each drawn in a specific order and to a specific form. Thus calligraphy offers preordained types of gesturality, and kanji—like those abstract works created by similar techniques—constitute a sort of visual force field, traces of the very gestures that created these signs.[22] Of the three types of kanji—block, semi-cursive, cursive (*shin, gyō, sō*; formal, semi-formal, informal: distinctions that permeate Japanese culture)—the cursive form, likened to wind-blown grass, is extremely fluid and often characterized by a hyperbolic reduction of brushstrokes, a curtailment tantamount to abstraction, so that a kanji that normally consists of a dozen strokes might be drawn with only two or three, or even with a single continuous line, often making it illegible.

One occasionally sees visitors in Japanese museums and temples engrossed before certain calligraphic scrolls drawing kanji in the air, trying to figure out the ideogram

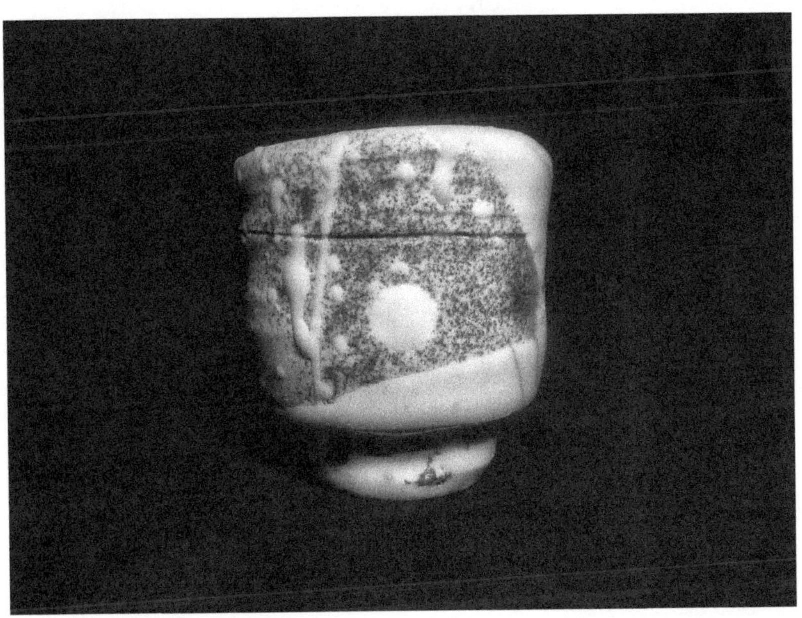

Guinomi *named "Night Snow," Koie Ryōji.*

represented by these all but abstract brushstrokes. The very fact that such calligraphic strokes are likened to swaying grass already suggests a level of equivocation—what one might speak of as visual metaphor—where the borders between abstraction and figuration, drawing and writing, representation and decoration, are fluid. These issues were played out in a very specific manner among postwar modernist Japanese calligraphers, for whom a radically new threshold exists between creating totally new forms of kanji and using the techniques of drawing kanji to produce spontaneous abstract images that might resemble kanji but in fact have no linguistic meaning. (This is not unlike the experimental potters working at the same time who made vase-like objects that could not serve as vases.) Kanji constitute both the cultural specificity and the formal limits of such works that vacillate between Zen calligraphy and non-Japanese abstraction.

We should remember D. T. Suzuki's comment, referring to the effects of moonlight: "The Japanese are lovers of softness, gentleness, semi-darkness, subtle suggestiveness, and everything in this category."[23] Like Leonardo da Vinci finding armies and forests, faces and figures in a blazing fire, in clouds, or in a splotch of paint on a wall—or like the "dream stone" landscapes that inspired Chinese painters, revealing the threshold between figuration and abstraction, or as the Chinese would say, between order and chaos— Japanese aesthetic vision emphasizes an imperative toward visualizing figures as they emerge from vagueness, ambiguity, amorphousness. One 11th-century Chinese painter, Sung Ti, proposed setting a piece of white silk in front of a dilapidated wall: "Then, morning and evening, you should gaze at it until, at length, you can see the ruins through the silk, its prominences, its levels, its zig-zags and its cleavages, storing them up in your mind and fixing them in your eyes. Make the prominences your mountains, the lower part your water, the hollows your ravines, the cracks your streams, the lighter parts your nearer points, the darker parts your more distant points. Get all these thoroughly into you and soon you will see men, birds, plants, and trees, flying and moving among them."[24]

Psychologically, one would speak of pareidolia, the perception of a pattern in random traces and forms, as in Rorschach tests or the man-in-the-moon (which is certainly culturally inflected, for the Japanese rather see a rabbit-in-the-moon), illusions that speak to the imperative to create visual order and meaning, what Gestalt psychologists see as the fundamental function of perception. Better attuned to such effects, the Japanese connoisseur is more likely to discern landscapes on irregular ceramic surfaces where the Westerner might find but a beautiful abstraction, and ceramic works with such effects are highly valued. As Okakura proclaims in *The Book of Tea*, well before Marcel Duchamp had the same intuition: "True beauty could be discovered only by one who mentally completed the incomplete."[25]

In traditional Japanese art, the ratio between illusion and allusion, between the seen and the evoked, between the visible and the invisible, is guided by the sense of *anji*, the suggestiveness that catalyzes the emotions and incites the imagination. A Japanese scholar once explained to Lafcadio Hearn: "The philosophy of Buddhism has a profundity far exceeding that of your Western theology, and we have studied it. We have sounded the depths of speculation only to find that there are depths unfathomable below those depths; we have voyaged to the farthest limit that thought may sail, only to find that the horizon forever recedes."[26] Every traveler must keep in mind this metaphysical warning against hubris.

In the West, it was not until the Romantic revolution at the dawn of modernism that artists would valorize the full pictorial force of such equivocal effects, and—in those decades before Impressionism—fully appreciate drawing as a form that leaves much to the imagination of the viewer, rather than finished oil paintings where every detail is precisely established. It is at this moment—not coincidentally when the air and water pollution caused by the Industrial Revolution first began to degrade the environment at a large scale—that atmosphere would become visible, substantial, transformative. Smoke, fog, mist, haze, steam, rain, snow, clouds, wind, floating dust, excessive light, even air and water pollution—phenomena that simultaneously make the ether visible and render things indistinct, even invisible—all trouble our vision and transform our view of the world. The concrete effects of atmosphere—including all sorts of optical distortions, as well as visual pathologies— would become prime aesthetic material, as exemplified in Impressionism. Ultimately, in Modernist and Postmodern art, smoke and fog, light and dust, mist and haze, would literally and materially become part of, or even constitute the entirety of, certain works of art: the ether would become as visible and as complex as the most concrete of objects, and certain crafts such as cuisine and ceramics would emerge from the smoke to take their place within the system of the fine arts.

On the limits of representation

One experiences a foreign city in hearsay and allusion, through literature and art, before ever setting foot in it. Upon reflection, I realize, with great astonishment, that until I first visited Kyoto in 2006, I knew absolutely nothing about the city, other than a few literary references, and it evoked no imagery whatsoever, besides that of the dry garden at Ryōan-ji. During the decades before I first traveled to Japan, I had seen many hundreds if not thousands of photographs of Ryōan-ji. None of them, however beautiful, however precise, prepared me for my first experience of the dry garden of that temple, which came as a shock. I was simultaneously stunned by its imperfect perfection and disconcerted to realize the limitations of photographic

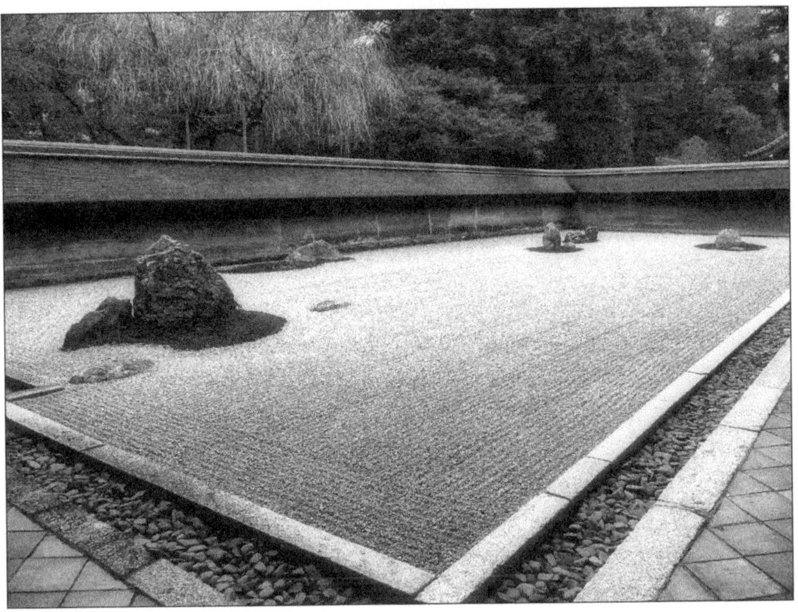

Ryōan-ji.

reproduction, as the garden appeared unlike any images I had seen of it.

Of course, the image is not the thing, and art is a transformation of the visible. My writing on Japan began with the project to document my stupefaction in a piece to be titled "Thirteen Errors in Viewing Ryōan-ji." This is not merely an instantiation of the fact that representation falls short of reality—which is a trite and misleading observation, because representation also transforms reality, and often enhances it—but it also suggests that our preparations for travel often take place in the realm of the fantastic. I shall thus discuss a representation of Ryōan-ji so extreme that it would be difficult not to speak of it as a misrepresentation. But of course, another word for misrepresentation is metaphor, which is what makes both creativity and recognition possible.

Consider an extreme example of how allusion can be constructed in relation to landscape, at the very limits of minimalism and abstraction. John Cage loved the dry garden of Ryōan-ji from the moment he saw it during his first trip to Japan in 1962. This places him in the lineage of great modernists inspired by this garden, including architect and urban planner Bruno Taut, whose appreciation of Ryōan-ji in the context of Western modernism inaugurated its discovery by the West and its rediscovery by the Japanese themselves. Another great architect, Philip Johnson, is said to have burst into tears upon seeing the garden. One of the most extreme, abstract, abstruse representations of Ryōan-ji is the series of drawings and engravings that John Cage began producing in 1983, entitled *Where R = Ryoanji*, inspired by the fifteen stones of the Ryōan-ji garden. These works consist of the sketched outlines of fifteen small stones from his collection: chance operations determine the choice of each stone, its placement on the paper, the type of pencil used to draw the outline, the number of times each stone is outlined, and the total number of outlines drawn. The only invariables are the dimensions of the paper and the particular fifteen stones that are used. The result is a seeming jumble of irregularly drawn and mostly overlapping circles on a blank background.

The fundamental intuition for these drawings is Cage's radical—and one might say eccentric, if not downright contentious—claim concerning the garden at Ryōan-ji: "I told him that I thought those stones could have been anywhere in that space, that I doubted whether their relationship was a planned one, that the emptiness of the sand was such

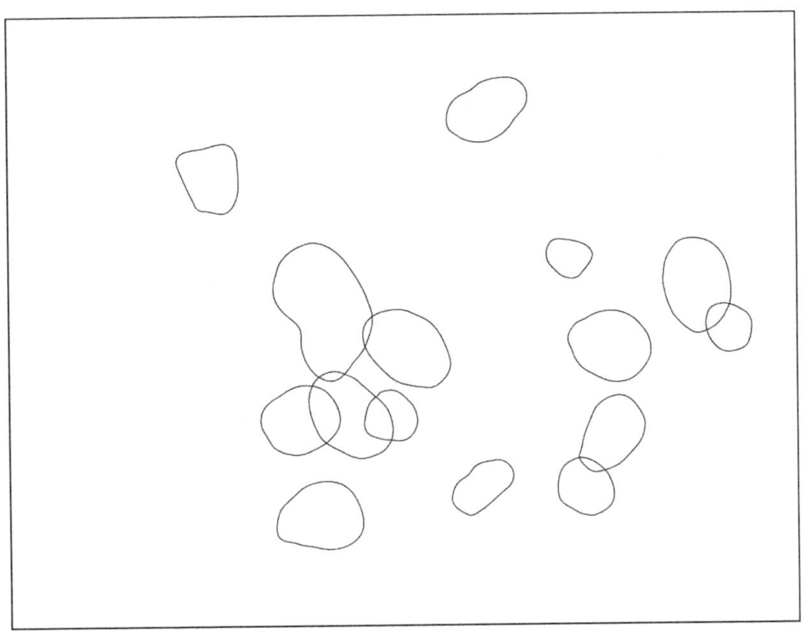

Allen S. Weiss, Ryoanji, Homage to John Cage *(2020).*

that it could support stones at any points in it."[27] Might this suggest an aesthetic primacy of the ineluctable, unchanging existence of the stones themselves, as opposed to the act of placement, which is ultimately an empty gesture? Or is the contingency of their existence overshadowed precisely by the performance of their placement, akin to a Zen gesture? In either case, for Cage any given form of the final design— of both garden and drawings—is acceptable, though provisional and ultimately beside the point.

Consider the differences between the garden of Ryōan-ji and Cage's series of drawings *Where R = Ryoanji* according to both the visual logic of the garden and the act of landscaping in general. The drawings resemble nothing so much as preparatory sketches for a dry "Zen" garden, a simple schematization based on two pre-given factors: the initial choice of the fifteen stones to be used and the limits of the ground plan. Here, the rectangular shape of the page roughly approximates that of the garden, and the number of stones *utilized* is identical to that of Ryōan-ji (though their forms greatly differ), while the final number of stones *depicted* varies. The rest of the actual garden's details (raked gravel, moss, walls, adjacent temple rooms, adjacent gardens, etc.) are eliminated. If the random placement of stones on the page suggests an elementary form of model (not unlike the Japanese art of *bonseki*, an interestingly formed stone grouping in a miniature arrangement), the pencil sketching of their circumferences reduces this model to a two-dimensional schema of a garden visualized from above, resulting in what amounts to a ground plan or an abstraction.[28] Between the actual garden and Cage's drawings there thus obtain transformations of material, form, dimension, scale, viewpoint. Furthermore, the stones of the garden at Ryōan-ji are set once and for all, while those of the drawings are perpetually replaced in the potentially limitless versions of this graphic work. The stones disappear in the drawings, and what is left are traces of the originary instant of creativity, the energy of Cage's hand in the act of drawing.

We thus find the *trace* of a gesture transmogrified into the *representation* of a garden. The semantic and symbolic content of the garden is nearly, but not totally, vacated in these minimal images. Does this suggest a new mode of landscaping, where the very form of a garden may be in perpetual transformation? (In a sense this is what *natura naturans*, nature as active principle, does to all landscapes, effecting their constant transformation.) Or is this series the ultimate extrapolation of the garden's imagery, a *reductio ad absurdum* confusing singularity with genre, such that *any* disposition of a given number of objects on *any* empty field would be aesthetically equivalent?

Cage clearly valorized the indeterminacy of the process over the determinate form of the object. Perhaps this situation arose because Cage identified with the gardeners of Ryōan-ji rather than with the visitors, valuing creative gesture over spectatorship. In *Where R = Ryoanji*, the representation of the Ryōan-ji garden exists in its most attenuated form, a mental image at the beginning of the creative process, while the finished works bear no recognizable trace of the garden. Cage demonstrated that he could evoke a mental representation and simultaneously destroy it in a single creative act. While realizing his hypothesis—that the fifteen stones could have been placed anywhere within the garden's limits—Cage effectively abolishes the representation of the garden.[29] We touch upon the extreme limits of representation, which necessarily provoke new ways of seeing.

◆ ◆ ◆

On 16 August 2016, the night of the Obon festival to honor the spirits of the dead, I received an email from my friend the philosopher Michael Lazarin, who resides in Kyoto within view of Daimonjiyama (in the Higashiyama mountain range), upon which a huge bonfire (*Daimonji-yaki*, the burning mountain) is lit this evening in the form of the kanji *dai* (大), meaning "*great*," stretching 160 meters wide. "It just ended. The mountain was cloud-covered; thunder and lightning; rain pounding on our verandah roof. Even if they could light the fires with jet fuel, it didn't seem that

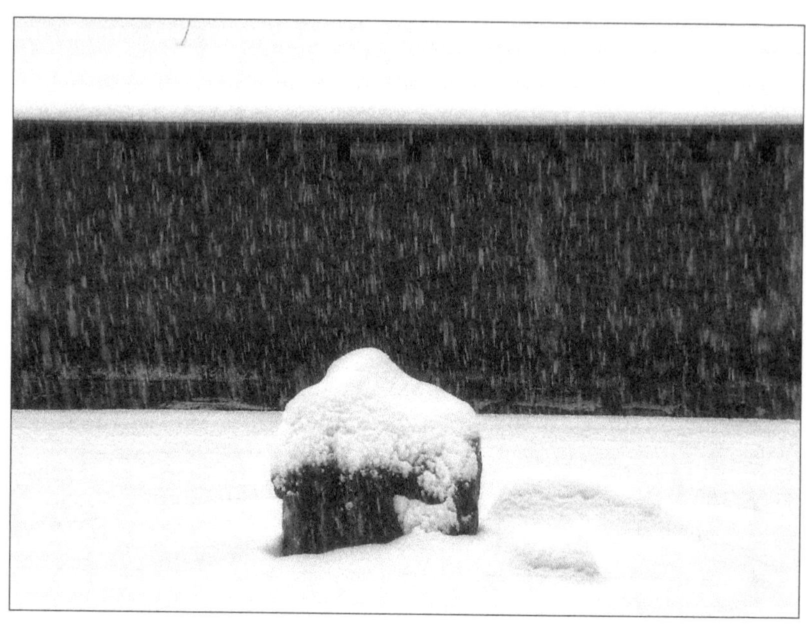

Ryōan-ji.

anything would be visible. Then flames licked through the clouds. Through the telescope it looked like a bank of clouds that one sees through an airplane window—with flames burning here and there. Very Buddhist. Then about ten minutes of Turner's 'Burning of the House of Lords' sky. Finally the heat of the fires burnt off the cloud and the 'dai' kanji was visible. Around the neighborhood, tourists who had been standing in the torrential downpour gave out a cheer. Because the mountain was obscured by the rain, the flames were very ghostly as they died down—truly memories of ancient wisdom drawn out of the atmosphere and back into the core of nothingness."[30]

The "Very Buddhist" is certainly ironic, for it is hard to imagine—however audacious the writer—that jet fuel and an aerial perspective could somehow be appropriately assimilated to the description of this traditional festival. And yet, stranger syncretisms have occurred in the history of religion. Nevertheless, the "memories of ancient wisdom" survive, emerging from an awe-inspiring atmospheric effect and fading into Zen nothingness.

5

Tanizaki's Tomb

THE CEMETERY

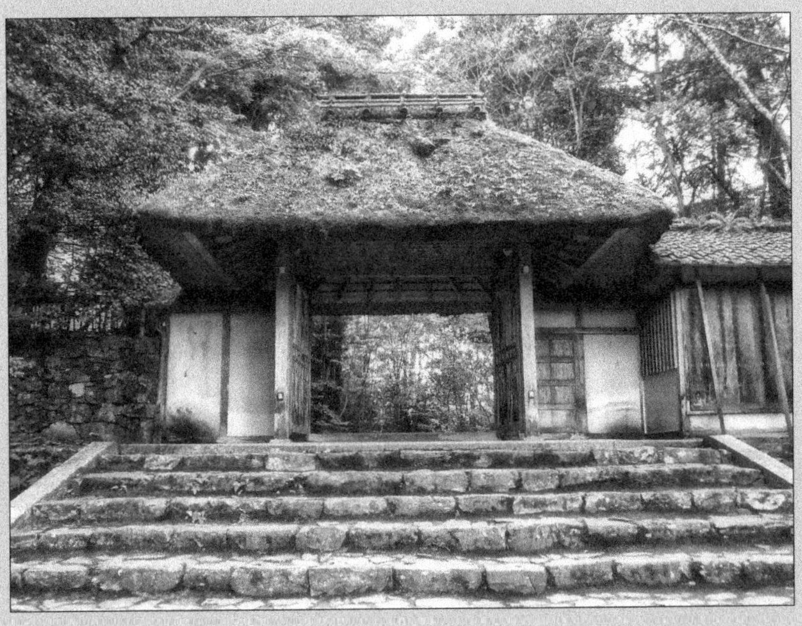

Hōnen-in.

*Arriving at each new city, the traveler finds
again a past of his that he did not know he had.*
  Italo Calvino, *Invisible Cities*

New Year's Eve 2015

In a way, the motivation to write this book is to do penance for photographing a bell, or to put it more precisely, to atone for not giving my full attention to its portentous peal. I was already attuned, one might say, to the great bell at Hōnen-in, since at midnight 2010 I had walked up the crooked snow-covered path that led to the temple so as to ring in the New Year and liberate the soul from the 108 passions that prevent it from leaving the circle of reincarnation, a necessary precondition of nirvana.[1] At that moment, from the vantage point at the foot of Daimonjiyama, with but a handful of people present in the freezing night, the sounds of the countless other bells in Kyoto were heard, as if echoing the one I had just tolled.

More recently, at midnight on New Year's Eve 2015, I ascended the same staircase leading to the edge of the forest, but this time the crowd was huge. The bell having already been rung the requisite 108 times, the iconoclastic yet generous abbot began a second round, defying tradition. Contrary to the solemnity of the earlier experience, this time the crowd was, while orderly, far from meditative. I took out my camera and, discreetly but assuredly, began to photograph the bell. What folly! To this day I still haven't recovered, psychologically or spiritually, from this metaphysical blunder. Every bell is a center that decenters. The slowly but inexorably decaying sound of a temple bell is simultaneously

142

movement and stasis, revealing—on the cusp between the sacred and the profane—the extension of space, the curve of time, the threshold of silence. One says that the sound of a bell "fades" or "dies away": the sound becomes as if progressively smaller, farther, past; such sound is the very incarnation of melancholy. This is tantamount to saying, in the Japanese context, that the chime of a bell instantiates a sonic mono no aware, the sadness of things that disappear. One might even suggest that the decrescendo of a bell is the patina of time, its sabi. My fateful photographs accomplished just the opposite: they froze time, condensed space, eliminated sound; they abolished the sonorous beauty of the landscape, and in doing so spurned ritual, ignored theology, degraded beauty.

◆ ◆ ◆

Alongside the canal parallel to the Higashiyama mountain range in eastern Kyoto is the Philosopher's Path (Tetsugaku-no-michi), so named because it was the route taken daily by philosopher Nishida Kitarō (1870–1945) on his way to teach at Kyoto University. This path, beginning near Ginkaku-ji (The Temple of the Silver Pavilion), passes beneath Hōnen-in and ends near the temple of Nanzen-ji. Midway along the path is to be found the temple Eikan-dō (Zenrin-ji), which houses one of the most beautiful sculptures in Kyoto, the sublime carving of Amida looking back over his left shoulder.

The origin of this curious pose is a moving theological fantasy. Buddhism offers sundry paths to enlightenment, including prayer, meditation, asceticism, pilgrimages, staring at a wall for extended periods, or even just sweeping a garden path. By modern reckoning, on 15 February 1082, one of the temple's priests, Eikan (also known as Yōkan, 1033–1111), of the Yuzu Nenbutsu school of Pure Land Buddhism, was practicing Nenbutsu, the ambulatory and uninterrupted ritual recitation of the name of the Buddha of Immeasurable Light and Life. This practice is believed to awaken enlightenment through the perception of the surrounding world in the form of paradise, and thus allow the deepest awareness of the emptiness of worldly phenomena. As Eikan reached the statue he suddenly stopped chanting, either from fatigue or sheer distraction, at which moment Amida Buddha turned his head to look back at Eikan, encouraging him to continue his chant. Eikan, overwhelmed by the beauty before him, pleaded with Amida to keep this pose forever, hence the name given to the statue, *Mikaeri Amida*, "Looking-Back Amida."

As the story is usually told, it is Eikan who is briefly immobilized, to be reanimated by the statue. But in fact, the profound poignancy of the tale is that the statue of Amida is animated by passion and mercy for just the instant it takes him to turn his head and address Eikan, to then strike the new pose for all eternity. A beautiful and wondrous symmetry: in but an instant, the motionless statue is moved because he who was in motion has halted, while he who paused then moves on because of the frozen gesture of the statue. The Pygmalion complex in a theological vein.

Confronted with the beauty of the statue and the memory of Eikan's experience, we the onlookers are also temporarily transfixed in admiration. It would be banal to mention that these days a sign stating "No Photos" has been placed in front of the statue, were it not for the irony that there is little chance that our pausing to photograph this figure will result in its sudden animation.

The freezing of time sometimes occurs suddenly, yet occasionally it is the end of a long process. Such is the very principle of painting, sculpture, photography. There are even those who would insist that the experience of collecting, whatever may be the object of desire, is one of removing the object from the flow of history and installing it in a timeless domain. One of the charming particularities of many Japanese temples is that they house collections, often of the most unexpected sort. In Kyoto there exist the famed moss temple (Saihō-ji, better known as Koke-dera), the cricket temple (Kegon-ji, also known as Suzumushi-dera), the Daruma temple (Hōrin-ji, alias Daruma-dera), the doll temple (Hōkyō-ji), and many others.

Probably the most beloved, and in Japan absolutely ubiquitous, of all Bodhisattva (Bosatsu in Japanese) is Jizō, a complex, syncretic figure, combining both animist magic and Buddhist theology: he is a local god of sexuality, fertility, and boundaries, replacing the animist border stones and fertility symbols previously found throughout Japan; he plays the role of a psychopompic guide through the underworld, mediating the realms of the living and the dead, overseeing transitional moments and liminal spaces such as burial and cremation sites; more recently he has been revered as the protector of women in childbirth, unborn children (for whom time is forever stilled, or one might even say for whom time never really existed), and travelers (for whom time is of the essence). Appearing as a monk with a walking staff, these tiny immobile monuments of stone are paradoxically often represented in motion, thus venerated by travelers and responsible for the pacification of restless spirits, as attested to in Noh theater.[2] They are to be found everywhere, often dressed in an infant's bib and cap adorned with red, a color that repels demons: on the grounds of temples and shrines, in public parks and at street corners, ensconced in the outer walls of houses and in commercial streets, and of course along the Philosopher's Path. Many Jizō were originally ancient phallic stones carved into figures of the Bodhisattva, often so worn down by the effects of the weather as well as by the beloved caresses of countless passersby over the centuries that they once again appear in their original phallic—or perhaps somewhat humanoid—form, often distinguishable as Jizō only by their bibs. As such, they are extreme manifestations of sabi, thus all the more precious.

To those foreigners imbued with the spirit of Friedrich Nietzsche's *Twilight of the Idols*, or who admire Alain Resnais and Chris Marker's film *Les statues meurent aussi* (Statues Also Die, 1953)—which reveals how ritual objects lose their religious and magical values when transposed into secular Western culture and consigned to museums—Jizō most likely appears today less as a tutelary deity than as enchanting little sculptures, or even more abstractly as another manifestation of the Japanese love of stones. For the Japanese, to the contrary, they are caressed, cherished, nurtured (occasionally with generous offerings of sake), and treated as if they were living spirits.

Yet it also happens that many of them are forgotten. The temple of Adashino Nenbutsu-ji, found among the bamboo-covered hills of the Arashiyama district of western Kyoto, sits on the site where in ancient times the aged were abandoned to pass away in the wind and the rain, and in more recent epochs where the dead were burned on funeral pyres. Thousands of statues of both the Buddha and sundry Bodhisattvas met a similar fate in those mountains,

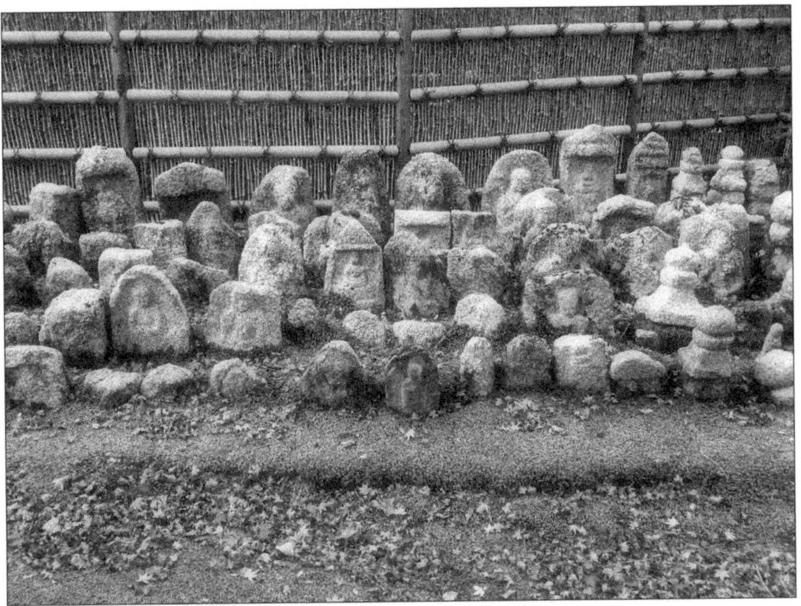

Jizō, Adashino Nenbutsu-ji.

abandoned and forgotten. Beginning in 1903, over eight thousand of these lost Jizō were collected and brought to this temple, an extraordinary memorial to the unknown dead and the forgotten statues. Colonial secularization and globalization have often resulted in the demise of local deities, as sacred objects devolve into works of art and rituals are transmuted into performance; but it is also true that certain gods die within their own domains at the hands of their very acolytes, from simple neglect.

There exists no place *simpliciter*; there is no abstract mathematical space on earth: every place is an intersection of crossing paths, a palimpsest of journeys, and a confluence of dead ends. The reality of space is a social phenomenon, a function not of intersecting lines but of intersecting lives.

The representation of space is always inflected by time, and there is also no time *simpliciter*. Time is not only a psychological phenomenon but a social one, which may best be described as "polychronic," a mix of different temporal dynamics marked by gesture, each with its own frame of reference. Such a complex means of examining time is fundamental to grasping the experience of gardens, where each flower and tree, statue and stone, insect and bird, exists according to a radically different time frame, not necessarily synchronous with our own specific and limited human temporal dimensions.[3]

Our perception of the world entails an inmixing of temporalities and spatialities: personal and historic, mythic and cosmic, quotidian and seasonal, ritual and functional. Existentially inaccessible to us, there is also a time of origins; an eschatological time (the time of the end of time); and an eternal time—the subject of theology, astrophysics, or science fiction. How is it that what best connects us to a place is sometimes the thing most solid, present, and seemingly immutable (like a stone or a sculpture of Jizō), and at other moments the most ethereal and ephemeral (like the fall of a petal or a leaf), and occasionally the most transcendental and eternal (like a demon or a deity)?

New Year's Day 2016

I awoke in the bed of Tanizaki's last muse. Well, in fact, it was probably not really her bed, as the mattress must have been changed numerous times since she last slept there. Nor was it really the apartment facing the path leading to Hōnen-in that Tanizaki knew intimately well, since the current one that I experienced was reconstructed some time after the writer's death. Furthermore, we'll never really know how far Tanizaki was able to take his obsession, and we must always beware of confusing life and literature. In any case, Watanabe Chimako, in whose former apartment I spent New Year's Eve, was Tanizaki Jun'ichirō's daughter-in-law, the model for Satsuko, the young woman whose feet were fetishized by the narrator in his final novel, *Diary of a Mad Old Man* (1961). His very first publication, *The Tattooer* (1910), is the tale of a tattoo artist who seeks the perfect woman upon whose skin he would create his masterpiece. His first glimpse of the incomparable beauty who would fulfill this role was of her foot: ". . . he noticed a woman's bare milk-white foot peeping out beneath the curtains of a departing palanquin. To his sharp eye, a human foot was as expressive as a face. This one was sheer perfection. Exquisitely chiseled toes, nails like the iridescent shells along the shore at Enoshima, a pearl-like rounded heel, skin so lustrous that it seemed bathed in the limpid waters of a mountain spring . . ."[4]

Eroticism, whether perverse or of more common varieties, is both intensely personal and culturally informed, thus one must not too easily dismiss George Bataille's audacious claim that "I challenge any lover of art to love a painting as much as a fetishist loves a shoe."[5] This in part explains the deep appeal, well beyond any formal qualities, of those photographs taken by Dōmon Ken in the ancient temples of Kyoto and Nara, focused on details of the sacred wooden statues that had been revered over the centuries for their spiritual qualities but now in a more secular age reveal the surprising sensuality of hands and feet emerging from the folds of clothing, not unlike the rampant sensuality of representations of the Virgin Mary during the Renaissance, when it was not unusual for a painter to grace the Blessed Virgin with the seductive features of his own mistress.[6]

So much Japanese culture involves dissimulation and the subsequent subtleties of revelation (miegakure): the moon appearing from behind clouds, a pine tree almost totally lost in the mist, a foot emerging from beneath a kimono, or that supremely erotic point, the nape of the neck, almost—but not quite—veiled by flowing black hair. In Japan, eroticism is rarely a matter of total nudity (the ritual of mixed public bathing, which was the norm until the opening of Japan to the West in the 19th century, made of such visions a common quotidian experience), nor of the celebration of the various curves of the body and the extravagance of gestures (since the kimono is a tubular form that flattens the body and restricts its motions).[7] While the poetry of the foot is not nearly as lyrical in *Diary of a Mad Old Man* as in *The Tattooer*, the fact that Satsuko, the object of the elderly narrator's obsession, is the fictional protagonist's daughter-in-law adds piquancy to the tale.[8]

Chimako was gifted the apartment in which I awoke on New Year's Day, where from the dimly lit bath I meditated upon this genealogy. The foot fetishism that excited Tanizaki from his earliest years, eroticism of a rather common sort, is intensified and complicated by the genealogical entanglements and quasi-incestuous perversity of Tanizaki's passion for Chimako. Such genealogical and erotic complexity was already evident in Tanizaki's previous writings, such as *A Portrait of Shunkin* (1933), the tale of two virtuoso musicians, whose relationship is simultaneously that of mistress and servant, teacher and pupil, and lovers; and especially in *The Bridge of Dreams* (1959), already written under the spell of Chimako, which is far more complex in its erotic complications: upon the death of the protagonist's mother, she is replaced by an almost indistinguishable double, who eventually supplants the narrator's natural mother in his memory and with whom he has an incestuous relationship, all the more troubling as he increasingly comes to resemble his own father.

It is relatively rare that one gets to enter the private precincts of a Japanese home, so if one sleeps in a stranger's bed it is advisable to know the broader circumstances. To enter a house is already to join its history, to sleep in one is to mingle one's phantasms with the spirits of the home. Writers love to insinuate themselves into narratives (and occasionally into a character's bed), often to the detriment of the novel. Readers are even worse. Just as the light was fading on this New Year's Day, I basked in a luxuriously hot bath, as Tanizaki might well have done numerous times in this same tub. One of the guests at the previous evening's celebration had brought as a gift a bag of *yuzu*, a citrus fruit whose grated peel is utilized as a flavoring in Japanese cuisine. They are also used for aromatic baths, a *yuzuyu* or *yuzuburo*, taken on the winter solstice, but in such matters I'm not a traditionalist and thus don't quibble about dates. However, this first bath of the year—with several of the fruit sliced in half, floating in the steaming water—had special significance, a sort of purification ritual before ascending again to Hōnen-in.

This apartment is hyperbolically bilateral but most asymmetric: built on a steep hill, the exposure of the salon gives on to a huge terrace and a vast panorama of Kyoto stretching out westward to the Arashiyama mountain range (the New Year's Eve aspect, lively and celebratory), while the opposite side, including the bath, is compressed at the foot of the hill leading to Hōnen-in, its mystically sonorous bell, and the cemetery where Tanizaki is buried at the threshold of the Higashiyama range (the New Year's Day aspect, withdrawn and retrospective). With the exception of a single tatami room, the apartment is resolutely modern and Western, a hybridism not unlike that of Tanizaki's novels.

As I steeped in the perfumed bath, I wondered about the symbolic transformation that I might be undergoing and made a mental note to see if there exists in Japan an ethnography equivalent to Marcel Detienne's *The Gardens of Adonis: Spices in Greek Mythology*, to grasp what effects the yuzu bath might be having on my body and soul. As the exposure of the bathroom is north and the window small, with the daylight already fading, the atmosphere was pure "Tanizaki," as he himself describes such experiences in his marvelous *In Praise of Shadows*, which I cite again: "We delight in the mere sight of the delicate glow of fading rays clinging to the surface of a dusky wall, there to live out what little life remains to them. We never tire of the sight, for to us this pale glow and these dim shadows far surpass any ornament."[9]

Its midnight sounds not yet diminished in my mind, the great bell at Hōnen-in rang. At dusk every day, the abbot of Hōnen-in ascends the earthen staircase that leads to the bell, to ring it twenty-three times in a slightly irregular and dirgelike meter, the peals—approximately a half-minute apart—punctuated by the occasional syncopated "clack!" of the *shishi-odoshi* (deer scarer) located at the other extremity of the temple grounds.[10] With the exception of the second and the final peal—each of which receives two beats in quick succession—every tone is allowed to fully decay before the subsequent sounding. I knew that I didn't have to rush, that before the bell would stop tolling I would have approximately twelve minutes—a small eternity—to ascend the path to the cemetery and pay homage to the author whose place I had temporarily usurped. I began to sense the nervous excitement of a ritual, where, as Ezra Pound and Ernest Fenollosa claim in their study of Noh theater, "the spirit is invoked and appears."[11] The bell rang again, this time a double peal that summoned imperatively . . .

An Intercalary Moment

. . . I entered the path leading up to Hōnen-in, as I had done at midnight to ring the bell, but today not a soul was to be seen. The dusk gave substance to what the French speak of as *entre chien et loup* (between dog and wolf), a transformative moment, the magic time of fairy tales. The evening resembled a wabi-sabi ceramic masterpiece: cold (*hie*), lean (*yase*), dried out (*kare*), those qualities that the legendary 16th-century tea master Takeno Jōō attributed to the greatest poetry: "It is said that the quintessence of poetry is a cold, dry, exhausted universe."[12] I ascended, as if the path were a *hashigakari*—that bridge on the Noh stage that connects the worlds of the fictive and the real, the wakeful and the dream, the past and the present, the sacred and the profane, the living and the dead—crossed by the protagonist during the opening moments of the play. I ascended, my body taken over by the successive rhythms of *jo-ha-kyū* (beginning, break, suddenness) that characterize all traditional Japanese performing arts. The bell sounds again. Like most paths in traditional Japanese gardens and landscapes, this one is crooked, and I am already elsewhere, other. I feel like the traveling priest in a Noh play, seeking an interlocutor to tell once again the tale endlessly told of awakening in the bed of an illicit lover, now long-departed, seeking absolution for my sin. The gate of the temple is shut, and I ascend directly to the cemetery, the stage. The bell sounds again. Time is measured precisely by these gongs. Time is protracted . . . or is it condensed? The cryptomeria loom above, the bell sounds again. The aged groundskeeper looks up from his sweeping to tell me to beware of the monkeys, who in this season bereft of visitors come down from the mountain to possess the domain of the human dead, confusing time and transforming space to create a world of demons, ghosts, and madness. I nod in thanks and begin to mount the stairs of the necropolis. When I turn around, he is gone. The bell sounds again. The secular has vanished into the sacred as I arrive at Tanizaki's tomb.

I place a small bouquet of white chrysanthemums and three yuzu at the foot of his tomb, imagining his desire that his mistress would forever tread upon his grave, with bare feet if possible. I dream another's dream as the bell rings again. There is a tradition in Japan for a poet, facing eternity, to write a death poem (*jisei*). In the 17th century, Takuan Sōhō simply wrote the *kanji* for "dream" (夢); a century later, Shisui drew an *enso* (a circle representing the universe, or the void). Bashō claimed that any of his poems could serve the purpose, but he too finally wrote one:

> *On a journey, ill:*
> *my dream goes wandering*
> *over withered fields.*[13]

On Tanizaki's tombstone is engraved the kanji *jaku* (寂): stillness, silence, tranquility, loneliness, emptiness, sadness,

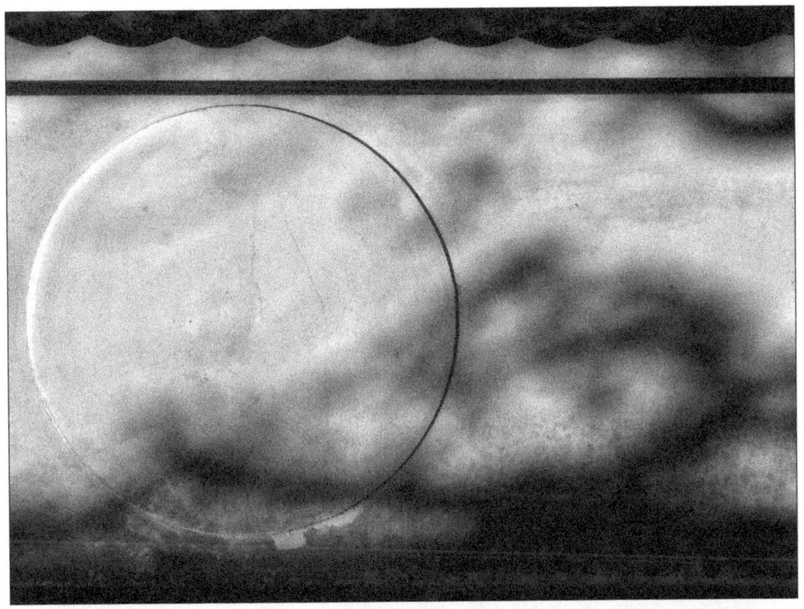

Monument to the "Guardians of the Imperial Tomb" (Gesshin-in, Kyoto): this monument commemorates the group of Imperial loyalists assassinated on 18 November 1867 by members of the military government; in Zen, the form of a circle (ensō) is a sign of both the void and enlightenment.

desolation; the alternate reading in Japanese is *sabi*. The genius of the language evokes a labyrinth of connotations, and consequently convoluted emotions. One is suspended between the infinite richness of Tanizaki's life, its distorted reflection in his writings, and the sheer nonsense of death. At this moment, his entire lexicon, his literary imagination, his very life, are all set in stone. This single kanji—suspended over the cemetery of Hōnen-in, over the Terrazza apartment, over the ancient city of Kyoto and the setting sun—is tantamount to Tanizaki's death poem. The bell sounds again. I imagine the classic shakuhachi tune, *A Bell Ringing in the Empty Sky.*

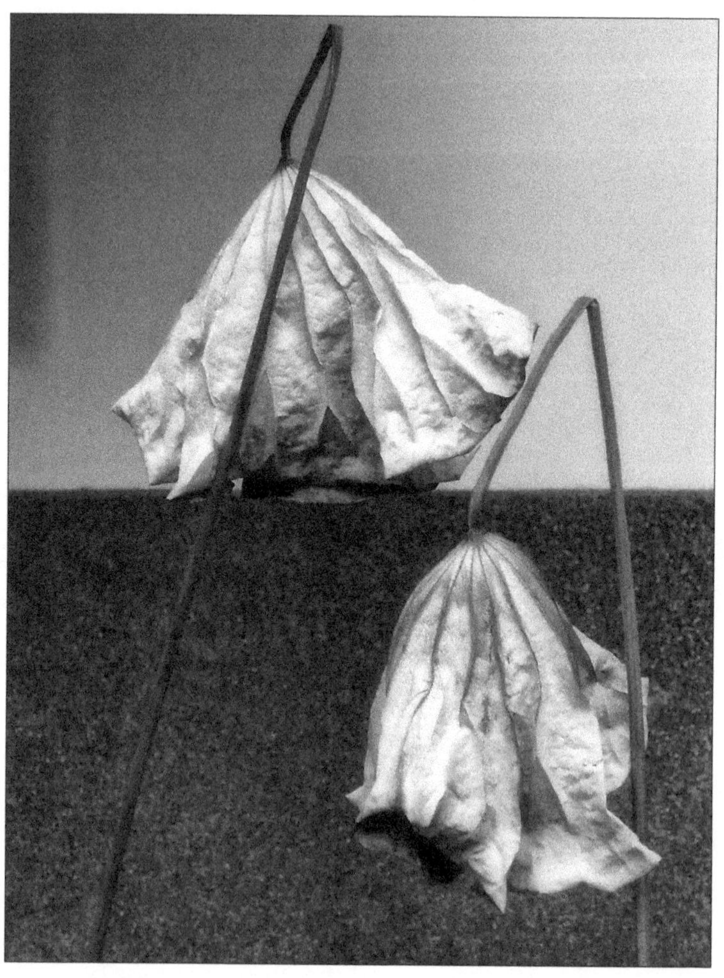

Lotus, Hōnen-in.

One of the most sublime moments in world literature is found in Murasaki Shikibu's *The Tale of Genji* (c. 1021), the supreme Japanese classic translated by Tanizaki into modern Japanese. The chapter dedicated to Genji's death is titled *Kumogakure*, "vanished behind the clouds": it con-sists of a blank page. Stillness, silence, sadness: jaku. The last glimmers of twilight color the Arashiyama range as the sun moves toward the Western Paradise. Centuries of psychopompomania, the madness of wishing to transport the dead to their eternal abode, connect Tanizaki's tomb to the disappearing solar globe in the land of the setting sun. Should one pray for his eternal repose, or celebrate his perverse fantasies? The evening would paradoxically last all night, animated by the artificial lights of Kyoto that surrep-titiously replace the daystar. The bell sounds again. I don't know how long I stood there, or how many more times the bell tolled. A troupe of monkeys descends from the forest angrily shaking branches, screaming, threatening. The last chime, two strokes, resounds. Then silence . . .

It has been said that in Western drama something hap-pens, while in Noh someone appears.[14] But I was the only one present. . . .

ENDNOTES

Epigraph

Matsuo Bashō, *Record of an Unreal Dwelling* (1690); *Genjūan no Ki*), cited in Haruo Shirane, *Traces of Dreams: Landscape, Cultural Memory, and the Poetry of Bashō* (Stanford: Stanford University Press, 1998), 92; cf. alternate translation in Makoto Ueda, *Matsuo Bashō* (Tokyo: Kodansha International, 1970), 121: "I believe there is no place in this world that is not an unreal dwelling."

Preface

---

1   René de Ceccatty, "Lettres de Tokyo," *Discordance*, no. 1 (1978), 99: "Découvrir une terre c'est d'abord rassembler les souvenirs qui l'annonçaient."

2   James Freeman, "Just One Thing After Another," *Impressions: The Journal of the Japanese Art Society of America*, no. 39 (2018), 67.

3   Donald Richie, *The Japan Journals* (Berkeley: Stone Bridge Press, 2004), 441.

4   Ernest Hemingway, *A Moveable Feast* (New York: Charles Scribner's Sons, 1964), title page.

5   Charles Darwin, "Introductory Note" in *Voyage of the Beagle* (1845; New York: Dover, 2002), 5.

6   Hans Ulrich Obrist, *Everything You Always Wanted to Know about Curating* (Berlin and New York: Sternberg Press, 2011), 100.

7   Jack Kerouac, *The Dharma Bums* (New York: New American Library, 1959), 157.

8   Gary Snyder, *Mountains and Rivers Without End* (Berkeley: Counterpoint, 1996).

9   Obrist, *Everything You Always Wanted to Know about Curating*, 33.

10   Needless to say, most serious travel accounts will in some manner discuss different ways of seeing, though often just incidentally. The closest to my project I have found concerning Kyoto is Alex Kerr (with Kathy Arlyn Sokol), *Another Kyoto* (London: Penguin Books, 2008): while the erudition is inspiring, the book is frustrating, as it contains neither footnotes nor any other sort of reference; an antiquarian and restorer of old homes, Kerr here centers on Japan's past glories but makes only passing mention of contemporary ceramics, and none of cuisine, two particularly dynamic art forms in contemporary Kyoto, not to mention dance of any sort, notably Butoh.

11   Olga Tokarczuk, *Flights*, trans. Jennifer Croft (2007; New York: Riverhead Books, 2017), 69.

12   Guy Debord, *Panegyric*, vols. 1 and 2, trans. John McHale (London: Verso Books, 2004), 74.

13   This relation between image and text is well expressed by Roland Barthes in his own book on Japan, *L'empire des signes* (Paris: Skira and Flammarion, 1970), 5: "The text does not 'comment' on the images. The images do not 'illustrate' the text: each one was for me just the point of departure of a sort of visual vacillation, perhaps analogous to that loss of meaning that Zen calls *satori*."

1   Equivocal Thresholds | THE TEA ROOM

1   Noritake Tsuda, *A History of Japanese Art: From Prehistory to the Taisho Period* (Rutland, VT: Tuttle, 2009), 39–40.

2   H. W. Janson, *History of Art* (New York: Abrams, 1969), 18–19.

3   Cited in Gregory P. A. Levine, *Daitokuji: The Visual Cultures of a Zen Monastery* (Seattle: University of Washington Press, 2005), 158. This book is an excellent introduction to the culture of the Daitoku-ji temple complex, the birthplace of the modern Japanese tea ceremony; see also Jon Covell

and Yamada Sōbin, *Zen at Daitoku-ji* (Tokyo: Kodansha International, 1974).

4   Michael Lazarin, email communication of 22 January 2019.

5   See Christine M. E. Guth, *Art, Tea, and Industry* (Princeton: Princeton University Press, 1993).

6   See Hank Glassman, *The Face of Jizō: Image and Cult in Medieval Japanese Buddhism* (Honolulu: University of Hawai'i Press, 2012), 120.

7   Kamo no Chōmei, *Hojoki: Visions of a Torn World*, trans. Yasuhiko Moriguchi and David Jenkins (Berkeley: Stone Bridge Press, 1996), 58

8   Ibid., 71.

9   See J. Thomas Rimer, ed., *Shisendo: Hall of the Poetry Immortals* (Tokyo: Weatherhill, 1991).

10 A replica of this hut has been exhibited at Kawai-jinja, a small shrine within the precincts of the Shimogamo shrine, which is where Kamo no Chōmei had hoped to receive a position.

11 Kamo no Chōmei, *Hojoki*, 54; see also Shōkin Furata, "Les aspects philosophiques du chashitsu, le pavillon de thé," in *Japon, Saveurs et Sérénité: La Cérémonie du Thé dans les collections de Musée des Arts Idemitsu* (Paris: Éditions des musées de la Ville de Paris, 1995).

12 Kamo no Chōmei, *Hojoki*, 76.

13 Kakuzō Okakura, *The Book of Tea* (1906; New York: Dover, 1961), 1; it is interesting to note that Okakura dedicated this book to "John La Farge *sensei*," thus acknowledging this American artist, enamored of Japan, as a mentor.

14 Ibid., 39.

15 Junichiro Tanizaki, *In Praise of Shadows* (Sedgwick, ME: Leete's Island Books, 1977) 8–9.

16 A. L. Sadler, *The Japanese Tea Ceremony* (1933; Rutland, VT: Tuttle, 2008), 30.

17 Tanizaki, *In Praise of Shadows*, 8.

18 Ibid., 8–9.

19 Ibid.

20 Ibid., 9.

21 Okamoto Tarō, "An Introduction to Tradition" (1955), in Doryun Chong *et al.*, eds., *From Postwar to Postmodern: Art in Japan 1945–1989* (New York: Museum of Modern Art, 2012), 67.

22 Bruno Taut, *Fundamentals of Japanese Architecture* (Tokyo: Kokusai Bunka Shinkokai, 1936), 10.

23 Okakura, *The Book of Tea*, 37.

24 David Pye, *The Nature and Art of Workmanship* (1968; London: The Herbert Press, 1995), 64.

25 Essential museums (all of which have published excellent catalogues) displaying tea ceremony ceramics include the Chado Research Center, the Nomura Museum, and the Raku Museum in Kyoto; the Sagawa Art Museum on Lake Biwa, near Kyoto; the Museum of Oriental Ceramics in Osaka; the Hatakayama Museum, the Idemitsu Museum, and the Nezu Museum in Tokyo; and for contemporary works, the Musée Tomo in Tokyo. There are several important collections of Japanese ceramics in the USA, including the Metropolitan Museum of Art and the Brooklyn Museum in New York; the Freer and Sackler Galleries in Washington, DC; and the Boston Museum of Fine Arts.

26 For a literary example of a dystopic tea room, see Cees Nooteboom, *Rituals* (1980; Baton Rouge: Louisiana State University Press, 1983).

2   Other Modernities | THE MUSEUM

1 This has been changing, however slowly, in recent years, led by the efforts of the Musée d'Orsay during the past quarter century to place the "decorative arts" on an equal footing with the "fine arts," a move subsequently followed by many museums worldwide. In this regard, the etymological and existential connections between *artisan* and *artist* should be remembered as a clue to the profound relations between art and craft.

2 See Allen S. Weiss, "Pop! Katsu," in Madeleine Schuppli,

ed., *Christian Marclay: Action* (Ostfildern, Germany: Hatje Cantz Verlag, 2015), 115–19.

3   Mukai Yumi, email communication of 9 October 2015.

4   Brian O'Doherty, *Inside the White Cube: The Ideology of the Gallery Space* (1976; Berkeley: University of California Press, 1986), 15.

5   Tanizaki, *In Praise of Shadows*, 9.

6   Pierre Bourdieu, *Distinction: A Social Critique of the Judgment of Taste*, trans. Richard Nice (1979; Abingdon, Oxon: Routledge, 1984).

7   To cite just two examples: the famed 16th-century Korean "Kizaemon-ido" tea bowl, claimed by many to be the epitome of wabi-sabi pottery, now preserved at Kohō-an (Daitoku-ji), as well as the oldest surviving *tenmoku* tea bowl made in Japan, dating from the 1480s and used by Ikkyū, now preserved at Shinju-an (Daitoku-ji), are both held in temples closed to the public and are extremely rarely exhibited.

8   On changing taste and art appreciation, see Stephen Bayley, *Taste: The Secret Meaning of Things* (1991; London: Circa Press, 2017).

9   See Christian Tschumi, *Mirei Shigemori: Modernizing the Japanese Garden* (Berkeley: Stone Bridge Press, 2005), and Geite Shigemori, *Shigemori Mirei: Creator of Spiritual Spaces* (Kyoto: Kyoto Tsushinsha Press, 2007).

10   Doryun Chong, *Tokyo 1955–1970: A New Avant-Garde* (New York: Museum of Modern Art, 2012), 105.

11   The Japanese passion for viewing maple leaves (*momiji*) well illustrates the culture-bound aspects of such passion. I grew up traveling through New England, New Hampshire, and Vermont every autumn to view the extraordinary display of the multicolored change of maple leaves, spread out over hundreds and hundreds of square miles. In Japan, multitudes of people flock to a relatively small number of famous sites to see the momiji, the red maple leaves (seemingly ignoring all the other colors of the season), and might stand ecstatic before a single tree. Objectively, both

qualitatively and quantitatively, these momiji can hardly stand comparison with the parallel natural phenomenon in New England; however, in Japan the momiji exist in a profound web of symbolic, artistic, and ritual significance: it is not the Japanese maple leaves themselves, but their presence in poetry, literature, woodblocks, and other arts that makes of them such a stunning experience.

12   Immediately afterward, Dōmon Ken, famed for his photographs of the survivors of Hiroshima, published *Shigaraki Otsubo* (1965), high-quality images of large Shigaraki pottery jars that would change the history of ceramic illustrations.

13   Gusty L. Herrigel, *La voie des fleurs*, translated from the German by Emma Cabire (1958; Paris: Éditions Arléa, 2019), 84.

14   See Akane Teshigahara, ed., *Sofu Teshigahara in the Postwar Avant-Garde*, vols. 1 and 2 (Tokyo: Setagaya Art Museum, 2001); the Sōgetsu site has a very useful timeline: https://www.sogetsu.or.jp/e/about/artcenter/.

15   See Dore Ashton, *The Delicate Thread: Teshigahara's Life in Art* (Tokyo: Kodansha International, 1997).

16   For example, the influence of John Cage was essential in inspiring Teshigahara Hiroshi's collaborator, the composer Takemitsu Tōru—who had long composed in Western experimental styles—to begin investigating traditional Japanese music.

17   Morikawa Kyoroku, cited in *Haikus*, trans. Roger Munier (Paris: Le Seuil/Points, 2006), 182; freely retranslated by the author.

18   Lafcadio Hearn, *Glimpses of Unfamiliar Japan*, vol. 1 (1894; Project Gutenberg eBook #8130, posted 18 December 2011), 352–53.

19   Chong, *From Postwar to Postmodern*, 99.

20   For a fuller treatment of this period, see Allen S. Weiss, *Zen Landscapes: Perspectives on Japanese Gardens and Ceramics* (London: Reaktion Books, 2013), 199–222. At the same time, Peter Voulkos was making similar innovations in the

USA; see *Voulkos: The Breakthrough Years*, ed. Glenn Adamson (New York: Museum of Arts and Design and London: Black Dog Publishing, 2016).

21 The Metroplitan Museum of Art (New York) has in their collection a related work by Yagi Kazuo, *Direction of the Wind—Unglazed Clay Pipe* (1955).

22 In 1960 MoMA, in the context of their *New Talent* series, had already given the most famous contemporary American potter, Peter Voulkos—several of whose innovations paralleled, and might have been inspired by, those of Yagi and the other Sōdeisha artists—a show of his ceramics and paintings. The fact that only sculptural, and not functional, works were chosen is indicative of the path that MoMA would take concerning ceramics. See *Voulkos: The Breakthrough Years*, 64–65. The very rare exceptions to this rule are pieces by those modern artists who occasionally worked with ceramics, such as Paul Gauguin, Kazimir Malevich, Lyubov Popova, Pablo Picasso, Joan Miró, Marc Chagall, Isamu Noguchi, Lucio Fontana. I say this less as a criticism than as a statement concerning how our aesthetic and categorical paradigms may blind us to the essential, and that these paradigms are filters of exclusion as well as inclusion. However, as I pen these thoughts the situation seems to be changing. One of the galleries at the newly opened MoMA featured six works by the great eccentric American potter George Ohr, placed amidst contemporary paintings of early-20th-century French masters, including one of the most beloved paintings in the museum, Van Gogh's *Starry Night*. Whether this is a paradigm-changing moment in the history of ceramics, or just a boldly eccentric curatorial gesture, waits to be seen. See Allen S. Weiss, "George Ohr at MoMA," *Cfile* (2020), accessed 16 January 2020: https://cfileonline.org/feature-paradigm-shift-george-ohr-at-moma/.

23 Dorothy C. Miller and William S. Lieberman, eds., *The New Japanese Painting and Sculpture* (New York: The Museum of Modern Art, 1966), 44–45.

24 Alexandra Munroe, "Circle: Modernism and Tradition," in *Japanese Art After 1945: Scream against the Sky,* ed. Alexandra Munroe (New York: Abrams, 1994), 134. One recent anthology makes this perfectly clear: "the book does not include texts on modernized traditional art forms— such as *nihonga* (Japanese-style painting), ikebana (flower arrangement), ceramics, and calligraphy . . ." (Chong, *From Postwar to Postmodern,* 16).

25 Consider the following anecdote as an allegory. I remember cultural critic Stephen Greenblatt speaking of the lost Shakespeare play *Cordelia,* based on a section of Don Quixote, that he and playwright Charles Mee recreated, to subsequently commission productions in several theaters around the world. He awaited the Japanese production in Yokohama with great anticipation, imagining a staging inspired by Kabuki or Noh theater. Instead, what he saw was *Motorcycle Don Quixote* (2006), a contemporary production in a dingy garage, with Harley-Davidson bikes and all. This should be a cautionary tale for all travelers seeking "tradition" and "authenticity," since tradition changes daily, and the contemporary is no less authentic than the ancient. See Allen S. Weiss, "Authenticity, or, the Paradoxes of Cuisine," *Cabinet* 11 (2003).

26 Aoyama Wahei, "Japanese Ceramics Now: Commentary on *Honoho Geijutsu* Cover Story and Ranking Survey," *EY-NET* (February 2004), unpaginated: http://www.e-yakimono. net/html/honoho-rankings-2004.html.

27 Ibid.

28 Sōetsu Yanagi, *The Unknown Craftsman,* adapted by Bernard Leach (Tokyo: Kodansha International, 1972), 178.

29 See Levine, *Daitokuji.*

30 See Jennifer L. Anderson, *An Introduction to Japanese Tea Ritual* (Albany: State University of New York Press, 1991), 95–109.

31 I was extraordinarily lucky to have seen "The 7-5-3 Garden" at Shinju-an (a subtemple of Daitoku-ji)—created by Murata Jukō, one of the founders of the wabi-sabi

tea ceremony, and said to be the prototype for the kare-sansui "dry garden"—through the generosity of friends who arranged the visit with the temple's abbot; and I was thrilled to have seen the magnificent series of fusuma paintings by Kanō Eitoku, as well as the garden that Sen no Rikyū is said to have designed, at Jukō-in, as a special favor I was granted as the recipient of a Japan Foundation Fellowship. While it is difficult to determine the motivations for such generosity, I believe that in part it was because I was believed to be offering something back through my writings. I regret, however, that I hadn't also thought of asking to see the Kizaemon-ido tea bowl, a National Treasure housed at Kōhō-an (also a subtemple of Daitoku-ji, and also closed to the public). This 15th–16th-century Korean rice bowl, repurposed in 16th-century Japan into a tea bowl, is considered by many to be the epitome of wabi-sabi tea culture and is rarely displayed in public (see Yanagi, *The Unknown Craftsman*, 190–96); the last public exhibition of this bowl was in Tokyo during the Nezu Museum exhibition of seventy-two rare tea bowls, *Ido Tea Bowls: Treasured Possessions of Muromachi Daimyo*, in 2013.

32 Yanagi, *The Unknown Craftsman*, 178.

33 Ibid., 187.

34 Ibid., 188.

35 Ibid., 178.

36 See Rupert Cox, ed., *The Culture of Copying in Japan* (New York and London: Routledge, 2008).

37 Two contemporaneous exhibitions suggest contradictory views of contemporary Japanese sculpture, differentiated precisely by traditional Japanese versus international modernist sensibilities. *A Primal Spirit* (LACMA, 1990) did not, despite its title, reference those Jōmon, Yayoi, and *dogū* (figurine) works at the origins of Japanese culture that so profoundly inspired the first generation of postwar Japanese artists, but rather featured works for the most part inflected by Shinto and Zen, such that "primal" signifies

something closer to "elemental," a connection with nature. All of the works exhibited were either made with natural materials or displayed in a natural setting, thus the elemental here signifies something site-specifically Japanese. To the contrary, *Against Nature* (Grey Art Gallery, 1989) was a typically postmodern exhibition, featuring conceptual and mixed media art of internationalist tendencies: urban works, made for the gallery, not the forest or field (as the title suggests). Indeed, if the artists' names were withheld, one would be hard pressed to guess the country of origin of many of these works, and several of the artists included specifically argue against any "Japaneseness" that can be deduced from their art. And yet, just as many of the works in *Primal Spirit* are indebted not only to their Zen and Shinto antecedents, but also inspired by land-art creators such as Robert Smithson, Michael Heier, Richard Long, and Andy Goldsworthy, many of the works in *Against Nature* that appear to be manifestations of contemporary international modernism cannot, however, be deciphered without explicit knowledge of their specific Japanese characteristics and situatedness. See Howard N. Fox, ed., *A Primal Spirit: Ten Contemporary Japanese Sculptors* (Los Angeles: Los Angeles County Museum of Art, 1990), and Kathy Halbreich *et al.*, eds., *Against Nature: Japanese Art in the Eighties* (New York: Grey Art Gallery, 1989).

38 Yanagi, *The Unknown Craftsman*, 178.

39 Early in 2020 the collector Louise Rosenfeld donated a diverse collection of over three thousand pieces of utilitarian ceramics to the Everson Museum (Syracuse, NY), with the stipulation that they be used until all but one piece is broken, and that the final, intact work be saved to tell the story of the collection.

40 Hans Ulrich Obrist, *Ways of Curating* (New York: Faber and Faber, 2014), 39.

41 See Allen S. Weiss, *The Grain of the Clay: Reflections on Ceramics and the Art of Collecting* (London: Reaktion Books, 2016), 180–84.

42 Ming Tiampo and Alexandra Munroe, *Gutai: Splendid Play-ground* (New York: Guggenheim Museum, 2013), 146–47.

43 André Lepecki, "Sous ses pieds la toile," in Jean-Michel Bouhours, Nathalie Rosticher, and Allen S. Weiss, eds., *Acte I: pour un nouveau musée* (Paris, Nouveau Musée national de Monaco / Éditions de La Martinière, 2004), 136.

44 Koie Ryōji, cited in Isabella Smith, "In praise of Ryoji Koie, the enfant terrible of Japanese ceramics," *Apollo* (International Art Magazine), 24 September 2020, accessed 27 December 2020: https://www.apollo-magazine.com/ryoji-koie-ceramic-artist-tribute.

45 Edmund de Waal, "High Unseriousness: Artists and Clay," in Simon Groom, ed., *A Secret History of Clay: From Gauguin to Gormley* (London: Tate Publishing, 2004), 43.

3   Perfect Offerings | THE RESTAURANT

---

1 Sei Shōnagon, *The Pillow Book of Sei Shonagon*, trans. Ivan Morris (New York: Columbia University Press, 1967): https://pressbooks.nvcc.edu/eng255/chapter/pillow-book/.

2 This situation is slowly changing; see, for example, ceramics created by Catherine White and Warren Frederick for the Japanese restaurant Omen in New York: http://www.sketchbookpress.com/omen/; also the current interest by restaurateurs in Danish studio pottery: https://www.nytimes.com/2016/11/15/t-magazine/design/danish-ceramics-kh-wurtz-mk-studio-lov-i-listed.html; and the increased use of studio ceramics in Parisian restaurants: https://www.nytimes.com/2017/03/29/t-magazine/design/pretty-restaurant-plates-paris.html.

3 See Kenji Ekuan, *The Aesthetics of the Japanese Lunchbox*, (Cambridge, MA: MIT Press, 1998).

4 See Allen S. Weiss, "In Advance of a Culinary Review," *artUS,* no. 33 (2012), from which this section is adapted. The finest study to date of the culinary implications of still life painting is Norman Bryson, *Looking at the Overlooked* (Cambridge, MA, Harvard University Press, 1990;

reprinted by Reaktion Books, 2018); see also Allen S. Weiss, *Feast and Folly: Cuisine, Intoxication, and the Poetics of the Sublime* (Albany, NY: State University of New York Press, 2002).

5   Michel Thévoz, *Pathologie du cadre* (Paris: Édition du Minuit, 2020), 136.

6   Ibid.

7   Kaichi Tsuji, *Kaiseki: Zen Tastes in Japanese Cooking* (Tokyo: Kodansha International, 1972); the French version was published in 1973. Chef Daniel Boulud first suggested that I consult this book, insisting on its prime importance in the history of French cuisine. The fact that this book was prefaced by Nobel Prize laureate Kawabata Yasunari and by Hayashiya Seizō, then Chief Curator of Ceramics at the Tokyo National Museum, and introduced by Sen Sōshitsu, a descendent of Sen no Rikyū and fifteenth-generation head of the Urasenke tea school, gives an idea of the importance of the publication. Among the many other volumes on the topic, see also: Yoshio Tsuchiya, *The Fine Art of Japanese Food Arrangement* (Tokyo: Kodansha International, 1985); Hisayuki Takeuchi, *Nouvelle Cuisine Japonaise* (Paris: Agnès Viénot, 2003); Yoshihiro Murata, *Kaiseki: The Exquisite Cuisine of Kyoto's Kikunoi Restaurant* (Tokyo: Kodansha International, 2006); Yoshihiro Imai, *Monk: Light and Shadow on the Philosopher's Path* (London and New York: Phaidon Press, 2021).

8   Wallace Stevens, "Anecdote of the Jar," in *The Collected Poems* (New York: Vintage, 1982), 76.

9   See Charlotte Anderson and Gorazd Vilhar, *Gracious Gifts: Japan's Sacred Offerings* (Tokyo: Shufunotomo, 1999).

10   Dôgen, *Instructions au cuisinier zen*, trans. Janine Coursin (1237; Paris: Le Promeneur, 1994), 23.

11   Ryoko Sekiguchi, *Fade* (Paris: Argol Editions, 2016), 54.

12   See Weiss, *The Grain of the Clay*, 60.

13   Matsuo Bashō, *Sarashina Travelogue* (1688), in Sam Hamill, ed. and trans., *Narrow Road to the Interior* (Boston and London: Shambhala, 2000), 78.

14 Ibid., 78–79.
15 Ibid.

4 Untimely Moons | THE GARDEN

1 D. T. Suzuki, *Zen and Japanese Culture* (New York: Pantheon, 1959), 393.
2 Kerouac, *The Dharma Bums*, 177
3 Murasaki Shikibu, *The Diary of Murasaki Shikibu*, in Donald Keene, ed., *Anthology of Japanese Literature* (New York: Grove Press, 1955), 153.
4 Yoshida Kenkō, *Essays in Idleness*, trans. Donald Keene (1330–32; New York: Columbia University Press, 1967), 20.
5 *Murasaki Shikibu: Her Diary and Poetic Memoirs*, trans. Richard Bowring (Princeton: Princeton University Press, 1982), 133.
6 Ibid., 132, note 66.
7 Yasunari Kawabata, "L'image de Kyôto—tout au fond de mon coeur," preface to Kaii Higashiyama, *Les quatre saisons de Kyôto*, trans. Ryōji Nakamura and René de Ceccatty (1969; Paris: Seuil, 2003), p. 9.
8 Augustin Berque, *Le sauvage et l'artifice: Les Japonais devant la nature* (Paris: Gallimard, 1986), 24.
9 Ezra Pound and Ernest Fenollosa, *The Classic Noh Theater of Japan* (1917; New York: New Directions, 1959), 6.
10 David A. Slawson, *Secret Teachings in the Art of Japanese Gardens: Design Principles, Aesthetic Values* (Tokyo: Kodansha International, 1987), 13.
11 On musical onomatopoeia, see Allen S. Weiss, *Varieties of Audio Mimesis: Musical Evocations of Landscape* (Berlin: Errant Bodies Press, 2008).
12 Shigenori Chikamatsu, *Stories from a Tearoom Window*, trans. Kozaburo Mori (Rutland, VT: Tuttle, 1982), 97; note that the author's name contains the word for pine, *matsu*.
13 Okakura, *The Book of Tea*, 35.
14 Hans Jürgen von der Wense, *A Shelter for Bells*, trans.

Herbert Pföstl (Inverness, CA: Epidote Press, 2020), 56.

15 Ibid., 142. Compare the comments on music and landscape in Barry Lopez, *Horizon* (New York: Vintage Books, 2020), 183–95.

16 The idea of an exhibition on *Atmosphere* was initially inspired by curator Jean-Michel Bouhours' project *Fumées* (Smoke), conceived for the Tabakalera International Center for Contemporary Culture at San Sebastian, but unrealized.

17 Hearn, *Glimpses of Unfamiliar Japan*, vol. 1, 75. In a contemporary vein, Motonaga Sadamasa, a member of the Gutai group, created a work in Osaka in 1957 that consisted of directing smoke rings illuminated by colored lights at the audience; see Bruce Atlshuler, *The Avant-Garde in Exhibition: New Art in the 20th Century* (New York: Abrams, 1994), 189; also note the 1970 performance organized in Niigata by the avant-garde GUN group, *Event to Change the Image of Snow (Trajectory of Steps)*, where an area of over 100 square meters was sprayed in color, a work that disappeared in about thirty minutes due to the falling snow; see Reiko Tomii, *Radicalism in the Wilderness: International Contemporaneity and 1960s Art in Japan* (Cambridge, MA, and London: MIT Press, 2016), 126–30.

18 Hearn, *Glimpses of Unfamiliar Japan*, vol. 2, 463–64.

19 Annette Michelson, "Paul; Sharits and the Critique of Illusionism: An Introduction," *Film Culture,* no. 65–66 (1978), 84.

20 Gaston Bachelard, *L'air et les songes: Essai sur l'imagination du mouvement* (Paris: José Corti, 1943), 17; see also Allen S. Weiss, "Dematerialization and Iconoclasm: Baroque Azure," in *Unnatural Horizons: Paradox and Contradiction in Landscape Architecture* (New York: Princeton Architectural Press, 1998), 52–55.

21 Chong, *From Postwar to Postmodern*, 76; for example, pottery specialist Robert Yellin, in his *Ode to Japanese Pottery* (Tokyo: Coherence, 2004), has named a sake cup by Bizen artist Kakurezaki Ryūichi the "Cup of Humanity" because

of a tiny crack in the pool in the shape of the kanji 人 (*hito*, person).

22 See Munroe, "Circle: Modernism and Tradition," in *Japanese Art After 1945*, 124–37; it is interesting that the image facing the opening of this chapter is a ceramic work by Yagi Kazuo entitled *Circle* (1967).

23 Suzuki, *Zen and Japanese Culture*, 393.

24 Cited in Dario Gamboni, *Potential Images: Ambiguity and Indeterminacy in Art*, trans. Mark Treharne (London: Reaktion Books, 2002), 24; this is the essential work on the subject of pareidolia; for the background of such studies in Gestalt psychology, see Ernst Gombrich, *Art and Illusion: A Study in the Psychology of Pictorial Representation* (1956; Princeton: Princeton University Press, 1960); in a very different context, that of the psychopathology of expression, see Hans Prinzhorn, *Artistry of the Mentally Ill* (1922), trans. Erik von Brockdorff (Berlin: Springer-Verlag, 1968). There are many technical means of creating such equivocal imagery, notable among them those used in the engravings of Hercules Segers; see Huigen Leeflang and Pieter Roelofs, eds., *Hercules Segers: Painter, Etcher* (Amsterdam: Rijksmuseum, 2016).

25 Okakura, *The Book of Tea*, 40. A flow chart is revelatory in this regard: the catalogue cover of the famed 1936 MoMA exhibition *Cubism and Abstract Art*, which attempts to delineate the diametrically opposed yet intimately related prewar genealogies of geometrical and non-geometrical abstraction. One might be surprised to find in the upper left-hand corner, as the very first element in the lineage of non-geometrical abstraction, *Japanese Prints*, one of only four influences highlighted in red (the others being *Near-Eastern Art*, *Negro Sculpture*, *Machine Esthetic*); see Alfred H. Barr, Jr., ed., *Cubism and Abstract Art* (New York: Museum of Modern Art, 1936), cover image. On the scientific origins of abstraction, see Serge Lemoine, ed., *Aux origines de l'abstraction: 1800–1914* (Paris: Réunion des musées nationaux, 2003); concerning the spiritual influences on abstraction, see Maurice Tuchman, ed., *The Spiritual in Art: Abstract*

Painting 1890–1985 (Los Angeles and New York: Los Angeles County Museum of Art and Abbeville Press, 1986); one awaits an equally comprehensive survey of the influence of the decorative arts on abstraction, perhaps centered on Aloïs Riegl's influential study, *Problems of Style*, trans. E. Kain (Princeton: Princeton University Press, 1992). While it is a truism that 18th- and 19th-century Japanese woodblock prints were a major influence on incipient European modernism, they are generally discussed in relation to new types of *figuration* (Monet, Gauguin, Van Gogh, Fauvism), thus it is rather surprising to see such works designated as an origin of *abstraction*. According to the diagram, this lineage leads from Japanese prints to Surrealism, which abounds in biomorphic forms on the cusp of figuration, as in the haunting otherworldly landscapes of Yves Tanguy.

26   Hearn, *Glimpses of Unfamiliar Japan*, vol. 2, 667.

27   John Cage, *A Year from Monday* (Middletown, CT: Wesleyan University Press, 1963), 137. Cage's instructions for *Where R = Ryoanji* may be placed in the lineage of miniature landscapes, notably Chinese scholar's rocks (oddly shaped stones resembling fantastic mountainous landscapes) and Japanese *bonseki* (miniature landscapes based on similar stones often combined with *bonsai*); we find the banalization of these art forms in recent do-it-yourself tabletop "Zen" garden kits.

28   The aleatory placement of these outlines inevitably causes many of them to overlap, which would make it impossible to use them as actual plans for the placement of stones in gardens, since in the *karesansui* garden stones are not piled one atop the other. A similar problem occurred when Merce Cunningham began to use aleatory techniques in the dances that he choreographed to Cage's music: to abide by totally random dance directions would risk having the dancers continually run into each other.

29   The drawings that fix the abstract forms of the stones nearly voided of symbolic and representational content

were ultimately transmuted into a form of energy that we call music. Simultaneous with his creation of the *Where R = Ryoanji* series, Cage also produced a series of compositions based on the garden, entitled simply *Ryoanji*. The different pieces were composed by using the outlines of the same fifteen stones utilized for *Where R = Ryoanji* as templates, randomly placed upon facing pages of the score, with the pitches at the beginning and end of each line determined by random pairs of notes, and the total pitch range of the piece fixed by the specific register of the instrument in question. The result is a series of either microtonal or very fine glissandi—often less than a semitone in range—sounding either independently or concatenated to form simple melodies; since the same limited number of curves are reused, the form is vaguely that of a fugue; see Allen S. Weiss, "On the Limits of Representation: Ryōan-ji, *Ryoanji*, *Where R = Ryoanji*," *Resonance* 3, no. 1 (2022).

30 Michael Lazarin, Kyoto, email communication of 16 August 2016.

5 Tanizaki's Tomb | THE CEMETERY

1 I recount this moment in Weiss, *The Grain of the Clay*, 171. The great bell at Hōnen-in can be heard in the radio broadcast *Radio Gidayū*—a sort of musique concrète soundscape—by Allen S. Weiss and Ishida Daisuke, commissioned by producer Marcus Gammel at the Klangkunst program of Deutschlandfunk Kultur and the Elektronischen Studio der Akademie der Künste (Berlin, 2014). In the European context, see Alain Corbin, *Village Bells: The Culture of the Senses in the Nineteenth-Century French Countryside*, trans. Martin Thom (New York: Columbia University Press, 1998).

2 See Glassman, *The Face of Jizō*; for the many guises of Jizō, see the list at https://www.onmarkproductions.com/html/jizo1.shtml.

3   Allen S. Weiss, "In Praise of Anachronism: Garden as Gesamtkunstwerk," in *Unnatural Horizons*, 108–53.

4   Junichiro Tanizaki, *The Tattooer* (1910), in *Seven Japanese Tales*, trans. Howard Hibbett (New York: Vintage Books, 1996), 163. Note the resemblance of Tanizaki's opening image of the isolated foot appearing from beneath the kimono and the ultimate image of a foot appearing in the corner of an otherwise abstract composition in Honoré de Balzac's short story "Le Chef-d'œuvre inconnu" (1831).

5   Georges Bataille, "L'esprit modern et le jeu des transpositions," *Documents,* no. 8 (1930), 490.

6   See Rossella Menegazzo, *Domon Ken: The Master of Japanese Realism* (Milan: Skira, 2017).

7   See Ofer Shagan, *Japanese Erotic Art* (London: Thames and Hudson, 2013), and Timothy Clark *et al.*, eds., *Shunga: Sex and Pleasure in Japanese Art* (London: The British Museum, 2013).

8   The relationship between Tanizaki and Watanabe Chimako, Tanizaki's real-life daughter-in-law, is intricate. One would need to draw a detailed genealogical chart to do justice to this complexity, but I will merely schematize: Tanizaki Jun'ichirō married Watanabe Matsuko (an inspiration, among others, for Tanizaki's final fictive protagonists), who had two children from an earlier marriage: her daughter Tanizaki Emiko (adopted by Tanizaki Jun'ichirō) and her son Watanabe Seiji (adopted by her sister, Watanabe Shigeko); Watanabe Seiji married Takaori Chimako (who became Watanabe Chimako, on whom the fictive Satsuko is based). Her genealogy is furthermore interesting in relation to local Kyoto culture, but our concern here is limited to her fictive appearance in Tanizaki's last book. Thanks to Michael Lazarin and Shimizu Hitomi for clarifying this genealogy.

9   Tanizaki, *In Praise of Shadows*, 8.

10   While writing this section, I struggled with the description of the sounding of the bell, long undecided as to whether I should describe the event as twenty-one strokes

of the bell with two double strokes or twenty-three strokes of the bell with two of them very close together. I have come to imagine that this descriptive difficulty might in fact be a form of Zen kōan.

11 Pound and Fenollosa, *The Classic Noh Theater of Japan*, 91.

12 As dramatized in the novel by Yasushi Inoue, *Le Maître de thé,* trans. Tadahiro Oku and Anna Guerineau (Paris: Livre de Poche, 2000), 150; see Louise Allison Cort, *Shigaraki: Potter's Village* (Bangkok: Orchid Press, 2001), 127–82.

13 Cited in Yoel Hoffmann, ed. and trans., *Japanese Death Poems* (Rutland, VT, and Tokyo: Tuttle, 1986), 82.

14 Paul Claudel, "Nô" (1926) in *L'oiseau noir dans le Soleil levant* (1927; Paris: Gallimard, 1974), 215: "Le drame, c'est quelque chose qui arrive, le Nō, c'est quelqu'un qui arrive."

RECOMMENDED READINGS

With the exception of Murasaki Shikibu's *The Tale of Genji* and Sei Shōnagon's *Pillow Book*, the following essential works may be read in the time it takes to fly from Europe or the USA to Japan (though I would far prefer more propitious reading conditions), yet they will inspire for a lifetime: first and foremost, selected poetry of, at the very least, Bashō, Buson, and Issa; Kamo no Chōmei, *An Account of a Ten-Foot-Square Hut*; Okakura Kakuzō, *The Book of Tea*; Donald Richie, *A Tractate on Japanese Aesthetics*; D. T. Suzuki, *What is Zen?*; Tanizaki Jun'ichirō, *In Praise of Shadows*; Yoshida Kenkō, *Essays in Idleness*.

My sincere thanks for the help and inspiration to Jean-François Allain, Daniel Boulud, Shari Cavin, John Dougill, Fujita Atsumi, Fukami Sueharu, Fukumoto Fuku, Thierry Maincent, Christian Marclay, Joan Mirviss, Randall Morris, Mukai Yumi, Tom Rasky, Shimizu Hitomi, Sugimoto Hiroshi, Umeda Minoru, Umeda Mitsuko, Yagi Akira.

Sections of this book have appeared in different form as:

"On the Limits of Representation: Ryōan-ji, *Ryoanji, Where R = Ryoanji,*" *Resonance* 3, no. 1 (2022).

"Bells," *Kyoto Journal,* no. 100 (Kyoto, 2021).

"Versions of Ryōan-ji," Writers in Kyoto website (2019).

"An Intercalary Moment," in Jann Williams and Ian Josh Yates, eds., *Encounters with Kyoto* (Kyoto: Writers in Kyoto, 2019).

"Cold Wintry Wind," in Christine Shaw and Etienne Turpin, eds., *The Work of Wind, Air, Land, Sea* (Berlin: K. Verlag, 2018).

"The Wrong Moon," Writers in Kyoto website (2018).

The Grain of the Clay: Reflections on Ceramics and the Art of Collecting (London: Reaktion Books, 2016).

Zen Landscapes: Perspectives on Japanese Gardens and Ceramics (London: Reaktion Books, 2013).

"In Advance of a Culinary Review," *artUS,* no. 33 (2012).

ALLEN S. WEISS is the author and editor of over forty books in the fields of performance theory, landscape architecture, gastronomy, sound art, experimental theater, and ceramics. He has written extensively on Japanese culture, including *Zen Landscapes: Perspectives on Japanese Gardens and Ceramics* (Reaktion Books) and *The Grain of the Clay: Reflections on Ceramics and the Art of Collecting* (Reaktion Books), as well as *Le goût de Kyoto* (Mercure de France) and *Guide anachronique de Kyoto* (Éditions Arléa). He has been the recipient of Fulbright, Japan Society, and Étant donné grants, and is Distinguished Teacher in the departments of Performance Studies and Cinema Studies in the Tisch School of the Arts at New York University.

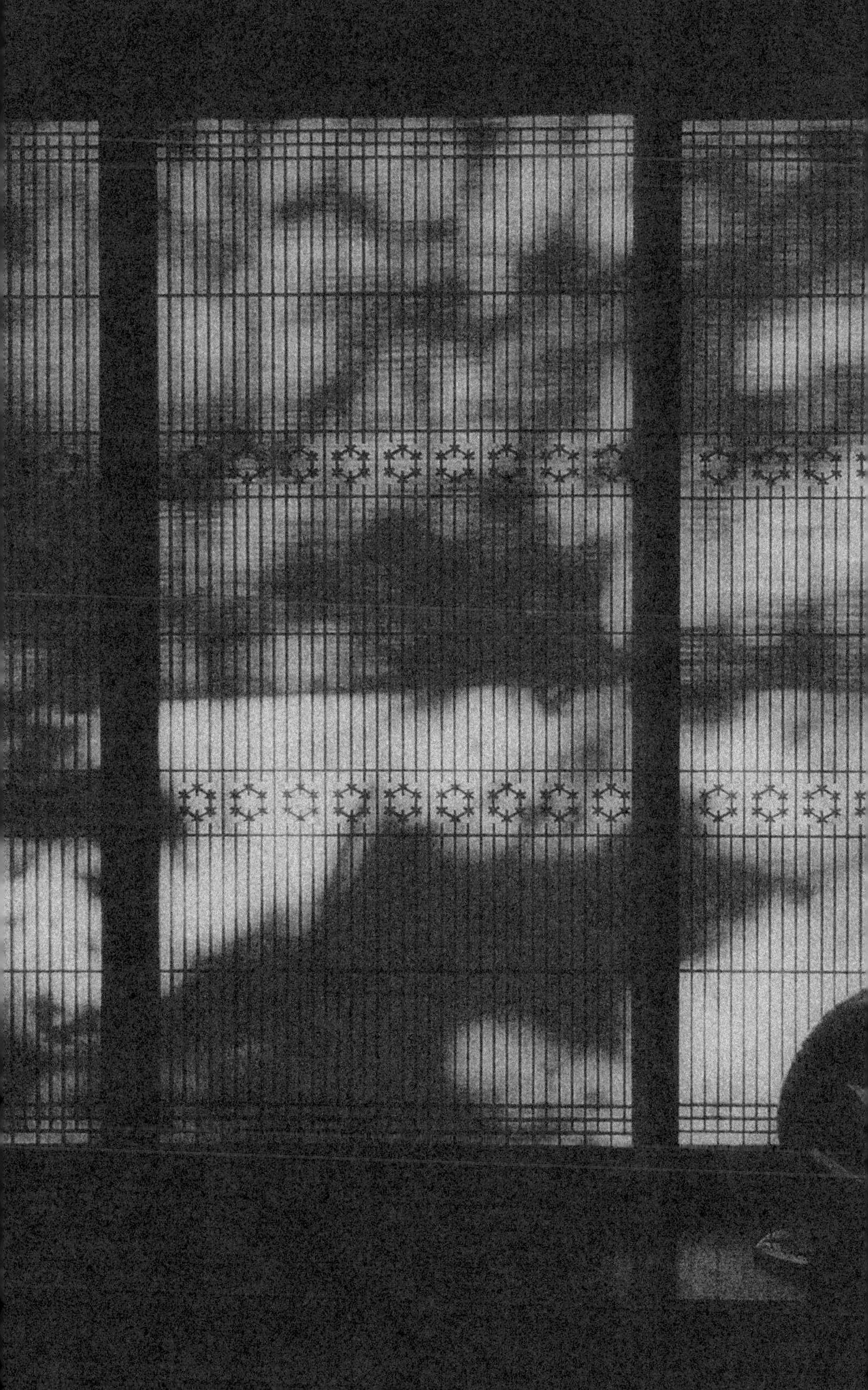

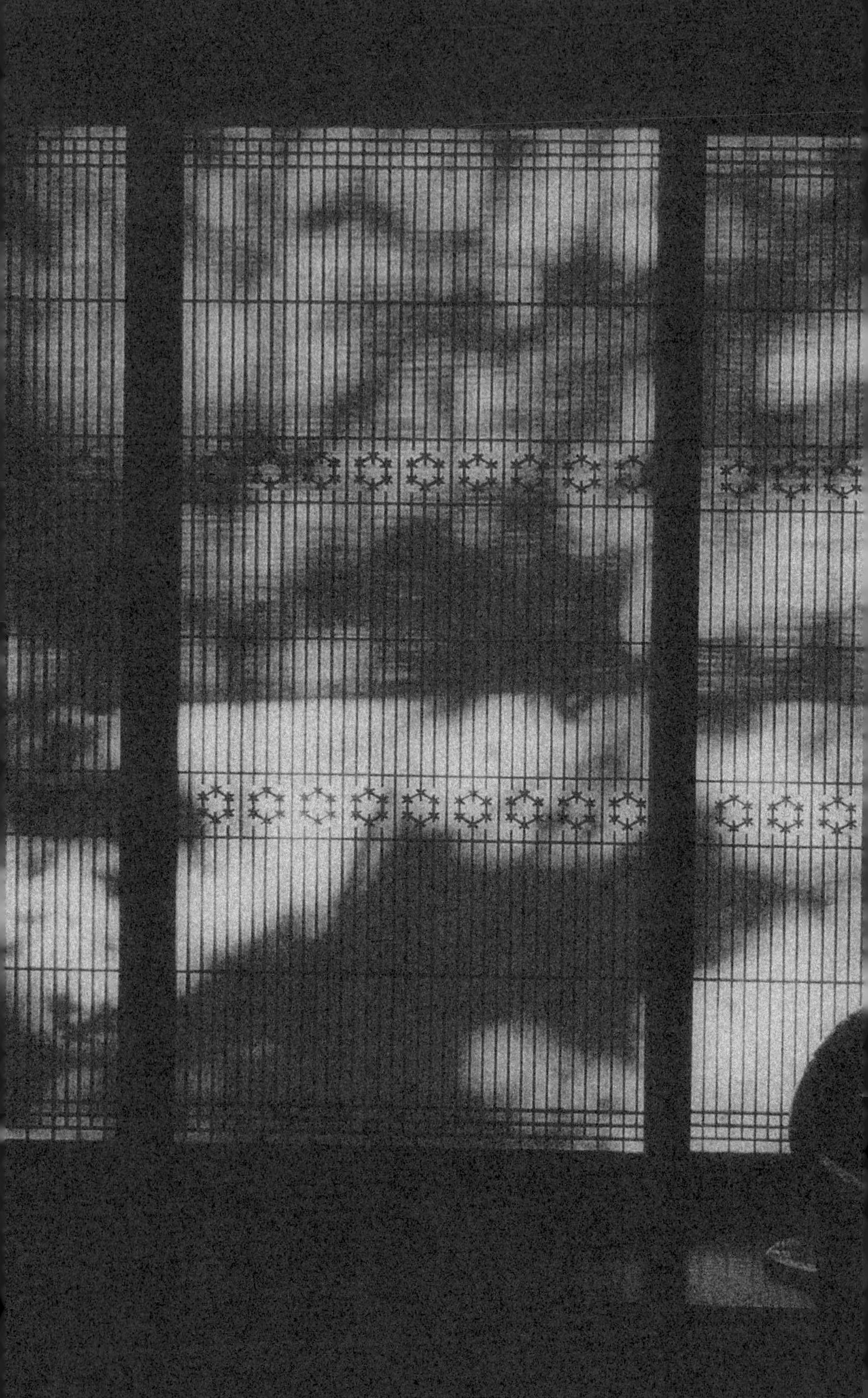